# NOBODY EVER LISTENED TO ME

## Stories and Words of Street Children throughout the World

### Compiled by
# DAVID MAIDMENT
## Co-Chair of the Consortium for Street Children
### (1998-2008)

## 'NOBODY EVER LISTENED TO ME ...'

A researcher, after each session with a child on the street, tried to offer some suggestion or help. After one four hour interview with a teenager whose life seemed totally wrecked, the researcher could not think what to say and apologised profusely that she could offer no help. The girl replied:

*'You've already helped me. You're the first person in my life who's ever listened to me.'*
*UK - Railway Children*

In an interview for the UN Human Rights Commissioner's report, a street boy said:

*'I can't think of anyone that I can go and speak to if I have a problem. No way. If I have a problem I just deal with it, I don't tell anyone.'*
*Morocco – Moroccan Children's Trust*

All royalties from this book will be donated to the Consortium for Street Children (CSC), www.streetchildren.org.uk, and those charities who have contributed to this book."

Previous titles:

Novels
The Child Madonna, Melrose Books, 2009
The Missing Madonna, PublishNation, 2012
Lives on the Line, Max Books, 2012

Non-fiction
The Other Railway Children, PublishNation, 2012

**Published in the United Kingdom by PublishNation**

ISBN: 978-1-291-16635-4

# CONTENTS

**Note:** All names of street children mentioned in the text
have been changed to maintain the children's anonymity.

# Preface

This is not a book for the academics or the practitioners. Its aim is to raise awareness of the realities of the lives of street children and give them a voice by telling their stories and quoting their words. One of the fundamental rights of all children enshrined in the 1989 United Nations 'Convention on the Rights of the Child' is that of participation, having the right to make your view known and taken into consideration in decisions made about you. As the girl whose words are quoted in the title of this book found out, street children do not often get the chance to exercise this right.

Some of the chapters, especially the early ones, make grim reading. But despite their experiences, the resilience and vitality of many of these children shines through and the later chapters reflect the potential when the children are given the opportunity. Too often the media paints a negative picture of these children and society stigmatises them. But it is often the most resourceful and strong children who reject the intolerable situations in which they find themselves and determine to do something about it, despite the risks and dangers that they incur.

The stories and quotations are drawn from three main sources – case histories offered by eighteen network members of the Consortium for Street Children (CSC) of which I was Co-Chair for ten years; quotations from two major pieces of research ('Off the Radar' (1) and 'Struggling to Survive' (2)) by the 'Railway Children', a charity I founded in 1995; and quotations from the 'Children's Voices' research paper written by the Consortium for Street Children's Advocacy Director, Anne Louise Meincke, for the Office of the High Commissioner for Human Rights as part of a report to the United Nations Human Rights Council in March 2012 (3).

I have added a short introductory essay to the stories and quotations in each chapter, to give the context of the children's experiences and words. The views expressed in these essays are mine, conditioned by the exposure I've had over the last twenty years of listening to my colleagues at the Consortium, the partners of Railway Children in India, East Africa and the UK, and talking to some of the street children themselves during visits to many of the programmes and projects designed to give street children an opportunity to develop their potential.

The term 'street child' was developed in the 1980s to describe any girl or boy for whom the street had become his or her habitual abode and/or source of livelihood and who was inadequately protected, supervised or directed by responsible adults. At that time 'street children' were categorised as either 'children on the street' who were on the street during the day and went home to their families at night; 'children of the street' who lived on the street without family support but maintained family links; or abandoned children who lived completely on their own. The UN Committee on the Rights of the Child has adopted the term 'children in street situations' recognising that children engage in numerous activities on the street and that if there is a 'problem' it is not the child but rather the situation in which he/she finds him/herself. The term 'street-connected child' is now used to understand and describe a child for whom the street is a central reference point – one which plays a significant role in his/her everyday life and identity. However, in this book, for simplicity's sake, the term 'street child' is used throughout, taken to include all the definitions of the term used above.

I would like to express my thanks in particular to the Directors of the various non-government organisations (NGOs) that have offered the stories and photos included in the book; to the staff and trustees of the Railway Children and their NGO partners and particularly to Emilie Smeaton, researcher, who captured the words of many children living on the streets of Kenya, Tanzania and the UK; to the staff of the Consortium for Street Children, particularly the former Director Alex Dressler and the current Director Sally Shire and to the Advocacy Director, Anne Louise Meincke; and to photographers Marcus Lyon, Dario Mitidieri and Robin Hammond who have all devoted their skills to recording the lives of street children in many countries.

**David Maidment**
**October 2012**

# Chapter 1
## *Why?*

UN Convention on the Rights of the Child, Article 2: 'State parties shall respect and ensure the rights set forth in the present Convention to each child in their jurisdiction without discrimination of any kind.'

**Photograph by Marcus Lyon**

I guess there have always been street children. There has even been reference to street children in ancient Rome. We are just more aware of them, or at least, we know now that it is a global phenomenon, especially as urbanisation has increased. We have always been aware of the orphans and beggar children on our own doorstep even if we, or the society we live in, chose to ignore them. It is not just an issue in the developing world. Charles Dickens wrote about the street children of London in 'Oliver Twist'. Today there are over 100,000 (4) reported runaway children under the age of sixteen each year in the UK - and many of these finish up living for a time on the street. We just do not call them street children. The situation is similar in Western Europe and in North America.

No-one has ever conducted an accurate global analysis of the numbers of such children although UNICEF in the 1990s made an estimate that ran into tens of millions - most in Latin America and South Asia, although in the last decade large increases have been reported in Africa and Eastern Europe, as a result of conflicts and the HIV/AIDS pandemic in Africa, and the collapse of communism and the resultant huge increase in unemployment in the former USSR state industries and its impact on the stability of families. The number of vulnerable children in many continents of the world seems to be increasing rather than decreasing as rapid urbanisation and large flows of immigrants result in the spread of slums with their inadequate infrastructure and high proportion of children.

Despite the fact that we seem to know more about them as a result of global communications and publicity from the number of voluntary organisations seeking to help them, we seem no nearer to providing all our children with the support they need at critical times in their lives. UNICEF, in a recent annual report on the state of the world's children (5) concluded that the UN Millennium Development Goals for 2015 were unlikely to be achieved for children in North Africa and the Middle East, in West and Central Africa, and in South Asia.

We do not, of course, know the real number of street children; indeed we find it difficult to define who is a 'street child'. Most children we label in this way are vulnerable and often destitute children who live in slums and favelas and who spend the majority of their days on the street attempting to eke out a survival by scavenging, begging or finding some informal trade opportunity to earn a few pence to bring back to their impoverished families at night. A small proportion - perhaps around 5-10% - survive full time on the streets, they work, eat, play and sleep there with, too often, only other street children as their companions and support.

And why are they there? Are they the 'Dick Whittingtons' of this age, seeking the 'pavements of gold' of the world's mega cities? Perhaps a few children are lured to the bright lights of Bollywood in Mumbai, or what they perceive to be their earning potential in Mexico City or Rio or Nairobi, but they are soon disillusioned. The vast majority of children who leave their homes for the streets are running away from situations they find intolerable or impossible. When Consortium for Street Children (CSC) was launched in 1993 at a reception given by the then Prime Minister, John Major, I undertook a risk assessment of being a street child - developing with the other member organisations an outline analysis of causes and consequences (6). To oversimplify, we found three immediate reasons for children coming to the street - they are sent there by their families to earn money and become detached; they are running away from physical, sexual or emotional abuse; or they have been neglected, abandoned or orphaned without extended family support to care for them. In 1993 a street children organisation in Mumbai (7) carried out a simple questionnaire with a thousand street children in the city. Most of the questions were factual, but the last one was, 'If you had just one wish, what would it be?' 90% of the children answered, 'To have a family who loved me.'

Most of these children are there, then, because they feel they have been rejected. Some people believe that the problem is just a result of crushing poverty, but rarely is poverty alone a cause for a child running away. Many have suffered violence in the home, at school or in their community. If you examine the records of phone help lines in any part of the world, you will discover that domestic violence and family conflict is the most frequent immediate cause or trigger of children running away - either as victims themselves or through the intolerable experience of watching their mothers or siblings being abused. The violence and abuse perpetrated on children within families and communities frequently is a result of the stresses and strains of intolerable living and employment conditions, ignored or unsupported by governments failing to live up to their commitments in Article 2 of the UN Convention on the Rights of the Child.

Other root causes identified by the risk analysis included the effect of natural catastrophes such as earthquakes, hurricanes and typhoons, floods, which disrupted the lives of children, orphaned many, made many more homeless and destitute. Armed conflicts and civil wars are further causes of vulnerable children taking to the street - as refugees, child soldiers, witnesses of atrocities affecting their families and communities, many children left to pick up the pieces alone subsequently. In the last decade 90% of casualties in conflict situations have been civilians, most children and the elderly (8). The ravages of the HIV/AIDS pandemic has rendered many children orphans, not just in Africa, but in parts of Latin America, India and Eastern Europe too. Under the strain, traditional child care by extended families has often broken down leaving young children to fend for themselves. And the teething problems of adopting capitalism since the collapse of communism in Eastern Europe has seen much unemployment and an increase in drug addiction and alcoholism leading to the neglect and abuse of children there, their removal to state orphanages and the fact that many children then vote with their feet over the inadequacies they find there.

Most people associate street children and runaways with teenagers - perhaps young teenagers. Whilst this may be true for some countries, particularly in Latin America and high income countries, many children are much younger. Many NGOs report that the average age of a child they find coming to street life in India is only eight. I have myself encountered children of four or five surviving without adult support and my own call to work for such children stemmed from being accosted by a six or seven year old girl on a Mumbai railway station who was whipping herself to arouse sympathy for her begging, exploited no doubt by an unscrupulous adult nearby. I have met children born and raised on the street, conceived by street girls who had been raped or succumbed to survival sex.

Most street children are boys, perhaps overall as many as 80%. But there are exceptions to this - in certain Indian cities such as Kolkata, surveys have identified nearly 50% to be girls (9) although most of these will still be attached to some sort of family. Lone children on the street are predominantly boys, although girls in this situation are the most vulnerable and sometimes disguise themselves as boys for their own protection. In some cultures, girls are better protected in the home, or are needed for household chores and looking after younger siblings, so the willingness to let girls escape to the street is lower. However, well-meant pressures to reduce the use of children in the sex trade and in domestic unpaid service has often meant that those girls have found themselves destitute on the street where no back-up development action has followed efforts to eradicate their previous abuse.

In some countries girls predominate amongst the runaway population - for some unknown reason this is especially true in developed countries. It is estimated that nearly two thirds of runaway children in the UK are girls. Recent research into the lives of children who spent more than a month living on UK streets when still under the age of sixteen [1], indicated that girls may feel more vulnerable when in abusive situations and are inclined to flee whereas boys are able - this is perhaps an oversimplification - to escape the impact of abuse by escaping to the streets with their mates during the day whilst remaining at home to sleep. In Western culture it also seems easier for a girl to admit that she needs help and take action, whereas for boys this is not seen as a 'macho' thing to do.

There is also evidence from a number of countries (including Russia [10] and the UK [1]) that a significant proportion of child runaways are fleeing state or private children's homes and orphanages. Children in such institutions are already often damaged by their previous experiences and are vulnerable to further abuse and bullying from older children and staff. Running away may seem to be a more attractive option to them.

Now let some of the children speak for themselves:

'I got a stepfather and found out at the age of fifteen that he wasn't my real dad and things went pear-shaped...And the worst thing was me finding out from someone else, not my parents. My mum lied to me - she said she did it to protect me. So I left home and was away for nine months. I got into the wrong crowd...they were into drugs.'
**16 year old boy, UK - Railway Children**

It was a normal hot and sunny day in Guatemala City. Directly across the road from me was a boy, probably about 14 years of age, slumped against a wall covered in posters of past concerts, rallies and the passing circus. His hands were squeezing a plastic bag containing glue. I walked over and sat down next to him. We sat there for a while before I said hello and told him my name. No further words were uttered as we both watched the traffic thunder past, now and again fanning the black smoke away from our faces as a bus drove past. Eventually the boy spoke to me. 'My name is Francisco,' he said. Little by little he opened up and then told me his story. Francisco lived with his family in the countryside. He and his father never really got on with each other. His mum would console him every time his father beat him. They were farmers and Francisco had always wanted to travel to Guatemala City. He had heard so many stories of life there.

One day Francisco was invited by his father to go with him to the capital and get some supplies. After sixteen hours on buses, Francisco and his father arrived in Guatemala City. They walked for a while down busy streets, arriving at a large supermarket. 'I'm just going in here to get some supplies,' Francisco's dad said to him, 'wait for me here.' Francisco waited, and waited, and waited. With tears in his eyes he told me how he had waited outside the supermarket for a whole week before he realised that he had been abandoned. Some days, people gave him food. Then a young street boy befriended him and took him to his gang. The boys taught Francisco how to steal, beg, guard and wash cars. Anything he earned or stole had to be shared with the group. That was one of the basic rules. Francisco also learned how to sniff glue and use drugs. His life as a street kid had begun. Now the school of the street was open for class and Francisco became a very diligent pupil.

**Francisco, Guatemala City – Street Kids Direct**

Angelique was born in Rwanda, near the border with Tanzania. Her parents were murdered during the genocide there. The organisation Streets Ahead Children's Centre Association (SACCA) investigated known prostitution houses in Kaborondo where young girls were said to be sold into the sex trade. They found Angelique who was only eight years old. She did not like to admit she was being sold and claimed she was living with an old woman who owned the house. SACCA took her to their centre. They discovered that after the genocide she had been living with an uncle whose wife tortured her when he was at work. When she ran away she was picked up by the old woman who took her to the brothel. Being a stranger to the area, Angelique had no choice but to stay and do as she was told. SACCA traced her grandmother - Angelique, now fourteen, studies at SACCA but visits her grandmother at every opportunity.

**Angelique, Rwanda - World Jewish Relief**

Turusifu lived with both his parents until they separated and he remained living at home with his mother. One day, aged nine, Turusifu was lighting the stove and the curtains caught fire. His mother beat him severely and told him to leave and live with his father. As he did not know where his father was, Turusifu lived on the streets in his home town, staying with a group of children who slept in video kiosks.

Turusifu's mother became unwell and moved to a larger town. Turusifu returned to live with his mother and helped care for her until her death. After his mother died, Turusifu was cared for by a number of women in the local area until he met his uncle who took him to live with his maternal aunt and grandmother in another town. Turusifu was then taken by his grandmother to his paternal grandfather in a rural area so he could attend school. However, after his grandmother left, Turusifu was beaten ruthlessly by his grandfather and cut with knives. He was forced to act as a herdsman looking after goats instead of attending school.

Turusifu found this maltreatment very difficult and went to the police, telling them he was an orphan and that he had a grandmother in another town. The police put Turusifu on a bus destined for where his grandmother lived. Once there, his grandmother told him to return to his grandfather and gave him the bus fare to return but Turusifu went to the town where he had lived earlier. He looked for, and found, his uncle who was an alcoholic and was unable to provide anywhere for Turusifu to live, so he, aged ten, came back to the streets where he has lived for the last seven years.

**Turusifu, East Africa – Railway Children**

'I was not in good understanding with my stepmother … When she gave me work to do – it's a must to do it; like washing utensils, fetching water. But then she used to beat me up; I got mark (scar) here.' (shown to researcher)

**Omega, East Africa – Railway Children**

When Ibada lived at home, his life changed when his mother died and his father remarried. His stepmother had other children and treated Ibada and his brother very differently to her children; she gave them less food and forced them to work on the land whilst her children relaxed. Her children attended school but Ibada and his brother did not. Ibada's father knew what was happening but did not do anything to address this.

'When my mother died, my father married another woman. That's when we began to suffer; to be tortured; made to suffer by my stepmother… Me and my brother decided to leave home and come here to the streets.'

**Ibada, East Africa – Railway Children**

7

On a positive note, many street children have strong characters and are particularly resilient to their situation. Some children are not ready to accept what they perceive as abuse, rejection or neglect and will select the dangers of the street as preferable to the situation they are fleeing. These children are moving from being reactive to victimisation to making proactive choices. Such children with initiative deserve support to fulfil their potential instead of becoming prey to those who would exploit them or lead them into criminal or further abusive ways.

# Chapter 2
## *Where?*

UN Convention on the Rights of the Child: Article 5: 'State parties shall respect the responsibilities, rights and duties of parents or, where applicable, the members of the extended family or community as provided for by local custom.... to provide in a manner consistent with the evolving capacity of the child, appropriate direction and guidance in the exercise by the child of the rights recognized in the present Convention.'

Photograph by Dario Mitidieri

In some places street children are very obvious, in others you have to search for them. If you go on to a large Indian railway station or into the slums of Kibera or Mathera in Nairobi, you will find them only too easily - they will probably find you first. If you go onto the streets of Edinburgh with the local NGO 'Streetwork', as I did recently, they will show you the haunts where the runaways congregate and sleep at night, but during the day the bus shelters or the graveyard above the tunnel over the railway lines cutting through the Princes Street gardens will show little evidence other than the detritus of discarded food wrappings and spent needles. In other locations the children will melt into the background and hide when police appear or other adults whom they fear or are suspicious of.

Where are the children then? Street children from the slum communities will be scavenging around their neighbourhood, rag-picking or collecting recyclable materials; they will be on the nearby crossroads at traffic lights or road junctions, dashing out between the traffic to sell you some cheap trinket or beg for the odd coin; they will have travelled into the city centre to seek casual employment, run errands, shine shoes, anything to earn something from the tourists around the posh hotels and restaurants, or carry bags at the bus or railway station, scavenge through the city rubbish dumps.

The lone runaway, abandoned and rejected children will be harder to find. Most will have learned to make themselves inconspicuous, fearful of authority in all its guises, whether a policeman, a railway official, an angry shop-keeper or hotel doorman. They are busy during the day on the move constantly, little entrepreneurs, never missing a trick, going where they see the opportunity to earn, or searching out the best places to get a free meal - from the dustbins of the hotels and restaurants, the left-overs in the otherwise empty coaches of a train that has completed its journey or a quick bite from an indulgent stall holder who they've just run an errand for.

They are in the mega cities of the world. This is where the activity is, where they can find the resources to survive. Many do not belong to the city, they are running from rural areas where their parents cannot cope or they have been beaten or bullied or have gone hungry for too long. They may start by being children from the city peripheral slums, hopping on trains and buses to the locations where they can make money, then gradually losing touch with home, staying to spend money they have earned on food and entertainment for themselves. Others may run to a local town where they meet with other children, then older youths tell them about the money they can make in the cities, so they try their luck and cadge an unpaid lift on a lorry or slip unseen onto a crowded bus or hide from the ticket inspector on a long distance train.

And it has become a familiar scene in cities in most countries of the world. For decades children have migrated to the streets in Central and South America. Brazil, Argentina, Guatemala, Honduras, Bolivia, Peru, Colombia, Mexico: these and many other Latin American countries have had an obvious street children presence for twenty or thirty years and now see second and third generations of street children. Cities like Rio de Janeiro, Sao Paulo, Guatemala City and Mexico City have street children too many to be numbered. The problem is so well established that gangs of street children are commonplace; they emerge from the slums and favelas and get involved with gangs of youths and link with other street children. All too often the police and other citizens cannot distinguish them from the young criminals in the gangs and they are caught up in the cross-fire of the efforts to cleanse the streets of crime (11).

Street children have been a common sight in South and South East Asia nearly as long. In Pakistan, Nepal, Sri Lanka, Indonesia, Thailand, the Philippines, but especially in India where estimated numbers range from 11 to 12 million according to UNICEF(1994) and the Indian National Commission for the Protection of Child Rights (2009). Of the latter, some 112,000 are arriving new every year at the major Indian railway stations (12) . Some, like New Delhi and CST station in Mumbai were receiving as many as 20-30 new children every day in the 1990s (13) , before the railway authorities, police and NGOs co-operated to contact and help the children before they were sucked into the abuse and corruption prevalent in those locations. As in Latin America, grinding poverty coupled with other childhood abuses render street children in this part of the world to be an endemic problem that no government action has yet been able to stem, let alone solve.

In Africa, the extended family culture kept the number of street children down until the spread of AIDS and the subsequent breakdown of communities under the scourge of the disease which has removed a generation of parents in many countries. The incidence of children orphaned by AIDS and unable to be supported by adult relatives has been exacerbated by the number of armed conflicts in several parts of Africa, particularly in Liberia, Sierra Leone, Northern Nigeria, Southern Sudan, the Democratic Republic of the Congo and Rwanda. Former conflicts in Angola and Mozambique have also left a legacy of detached and vulnerable children, as have the years of apartheid and consequent poverty and abuse of human rights in South Africa.

Communist governments in Eastern Europe controlled the street tightly and social policies put full employment as a high priority. In the last fifteen years such policies have been overturned and many cities in Russia, for example, now have over 50% unemployment especially where the workforce previously relied on the vast state industries and the defence budget. The Russian government categorises as 'social orphans' children of drug addicts, alcoholics and those whose parents are in prison, and usually places such children in one of the state orphanages. The Russian government admit to identifying 800,000 such children; many of these children flee from these institutions and 50% or more of runaways arriving in Moscow from the provinces are alleged to come from such situations (10). Russian NGOs estimate the real number of street children to be upwards of two million. Roma children in many Eastern European countries suffer discrimination and poor access to education and health care and form a high proportion of street children.

Lastly, the number of runaway children in the developed world must not be overlooked. The USA is estimated to have over a million runaway children and youth each year and the UK figure of 100,000 under 16 year olds includes a high percentage of children whose absence has not been reported by their carers (4). These children, estimated to be as much as 60-70% of the total runaways by the UK police, are probably at greatest risk. Once such children in the UK could be found concentrated in London, around the railway termini, Victoria coach station and the West End amusement arcades. Two captains of the Salvation Army who patrolled the London railway termini with a BTC policeman in a decade from the mid 1980s told me that they had picked up 3,600 young lone children and teenagers at risk during their evening rounds. The extra presence of police and surveillance cameras, plus the tightening of railway ticket barrier control, has meant that it's now harder to find such children, and many are dispersed over other cities - Leeds, Reading, Nottingham, Sheffield, Manchester, Liverpool, Edinburgh and Glasgow. It is said that Bristol now has the second highest number of runaway young people in the UK, and many can be found hanging around the city's bus terminal. Other places that become the home of such rejected children and young people are less expected. Prosperous tourist towns and cities have their 'sink estates' and vulnerable children escaping from dysfunctional families.

The children's voices:

*In one of the most dangerous zones of the Guatemala's city, where insecurity and abuse are suffered on a daily basis, José lived. A child of 12 years old, short, and with a small body, because of the inappropriate practices that his parents made him to do, José used to live with his mother and with his younger sister Maria. His father would come and beat his children.*

*'My little sister and I, we couldn't study because my parents didn't want us to, they said there wasn't any money but I know it was because they didn't care about us... my mother hit me and also my father,' says José.'I had to go out every day at different times because my parents forced me to sell drugs in the streets, and because I was little, nobody noticed it. Oh! But if I didn't want to go out they beat me really hard, well they also beat me when they were fighting because my father didn't live with us anymore'.*

*In Guatemala, children are constantly exposed to high levels of violence, there is no respect for their lives, they live in violence in their own homes and they absorb it and learn it. Some children are used as 'mulas' or drug carriers. The drug dealing, the people trafficking trade, weapons and prostitution are generating high levels of social deterioration and crisis that leads to frustration, according to the Programme for the Care, Mobilization and Incidence for Children and Adolescents (PAMI).*

*In January 2009, José was found selling illegal substances, so the Minors Attorney City's Office sent him directly to one of the Homes that are a part of the Guatemala Early Encounter. In there, children are provided for all basic needs and have a school to study, and they live in a harmonious healthy family home, however the procedures aren't easy to overcome. José had many difficulties in his adaptation process, because living in an unstable environment and surrounded by much violence, reflected the learned things when he related to others.*

*'... I didn´t know what it was like to live because what I´ve learned was to survive ...'*

*After eleven months, José has demonstrated a big advancement; he is sociable, respectful, he likes to study and has demonstrated positive leadership skills.*

*'Now I can say I've started a new beginning' said José with a smile in his face, '... after what I´ve lived, I didn't think I could do well, but now I can study and even though it is difficult for me, I will make an effort because I want to do things right; people love me here, they don't beat me, it is a new beginning for me, now I am ok'.*

### José, Guatemala City – Toybox

*Father Patrick Shanahan, founder of Street Child Africa, was visiting partner agency 'Meninos de Mozambique' in 2005, when he met a little girl called 'Mariama'. She was making her living on the pickings of a rubbish dump – as do many of the poorest children in Maputo, the capital city. At the age of 8, Mariama was the sole carer for three younger siblings - a 5 year old boy, a 3 year old and a baby. She was well known to the adults of the slums but nobody had realised her situation - they simply assumed that somebody, somewhere, was looking after them. She had slipped through the net. She was frightened that if the authorities discovered her they would separate her little family and place them in foster care. Having lost both her parents, the thought of losing her siblings was unbearable. Just imagine - an 8 year old caring for a baby, with no help. The extraordinary thing for Father Shanahan was not only her predicament, but her resourcefulness and resilience. We underestimate children, and what they are capable of, when we try to make interventions without consulting them first. Meninos worked with Mariama and her siblings to find ways of keeping the children together. Now, they are safe and still have each other and a carer.*

### Mariama, Mozambique - Street Child Africa

*A street child's greatest wish is to belong, and be loved as part of a family. Sadly, for many this is only a dream. Street children often come from difficult family backgrounds, with a history of abuse or family breakdown. Gaston, from Cochabamba, Bolivia, had a very difficult start in life. His parents separated when his father abandoned the family and went to live with another woman. When his mother committed a minor crime, she was sent to San Sebastian prison, and her children all moved into the jail with her. Whole families often live in prison in Bolivia, especially those with only one parent. There is simply nowhere else for the* children to go. However, during the day Gaston is able to come out of the prison and he became part of a Toybox supported local project where he gets food, education, a place to play, friends and adults to care for him.

Thanks to this support, Gaston feels that he belongs again. He has been elected by his peers as an Ambassador because he is seen as a leader. Now twelve years old, he is a mature and responsible boy, who is very aware of the value of family. He writes:

'My mum is very nice, I help her do things. She works in the jail doing laundry and sewing.'

Gaston is one of the Child Ambassadors at 'Casa de la Amistad' (Friendship House) – a project in Cochabamba, Bolivia.

**Gaston, Bolivia – Toybox**


Rose was born in Romania, is a Roma child and second youngest in a family of eight. When she was thirteen, her parents sent her to England as her brother was there, and thought she could get a job. She was smuggled there in a lorry, but when she arrived she found her brother had been sent back to Romania. She was given a room with other 14-16 year old girls, but she was lonely, frightened and intimidated by the behaviour of the other girls. At fourteen years of age she started spending time on the streets. She said:

'I slept one day here, one day there, sometimes I had to sleep at the railway station, in the park, at the bus station. I had to go out of London; I tried staying in Manchester... People will give me a bed for the night but they always want me to pay my share and I haven't got any money. I couldn't speak English; I couldn't communicate with people.'

**Rose, UK, Railway Children**


Ten year old Victor was abandoned by his parents who split and went abroad leaving him in the care of an alcoholic relative. The scared boy left his village, Kishinev, and began to tramp. For two years he lived in fear of being caught by the police after he stole a wallet to find money to survive. He arrived at a children's home in 2006 - although initially very obstinate and finding it difficult to mix with the other children, eventually he began to smile. He likes drawing and singing Moldovian national songs and dreams one day of being a car salesman.

**Victor, Moldova, World Jewish Relief**


**In conclusion therefore, it is easy to say that large numbers exist in most countries of the world, but often much harder to get firm statistics of the number of children 'of the street' or children**

out of school or in informal labour. It is easy for members of the general public to miss such children, especially if they become ingrained to seeing such children as the norm. It is not easy to distinguish between those children who spend the majority of the day on the street but are still strongly linked with their families and those particularly vulnerable children who are seeking to survive alone or without adult support of a positive nature.

# Chapter 3
## *Violence*

UN Convention on the Rights of the Child, Article 19: 'State Parties shall take all appropriate legislative, administrative, social and educational measures to protect the child from all forms of physical or mental violence, injury or abuse, neglect or negligent treatment, maltreatment or exploitation, including sexual abuse, while in the care of parent(s), legal guardian(s) or any other person who has care of the child.'

**Photograph by Robin Hammond**

Street children accumulate numerous experiences of violence from an early age and in a range of environments. Their experiences in countries across the world are strikingly similar - including those in rich countries with child protection systems, as well as those in poorer countries which may have weaker support systems. 25 years after street children first made the international headlines, governments around the world continue to use violent tactics with street children, which contravene their rights, exacerbate their experience of violence and scapegoat them and their families.

The world of violence and street children is complex. Street children accumulate a range of experiences of violence: children survive abuse at home in fragile families and this is often the cause of the first push towards street living; they live in poverty-afflicted, chaotic neighbourhoods; their access to educational and health services is erratic, discriminatory and exclusionary; they confront risks in the street, experiencing violence in their premature entry into the world of work; they are subjected to abuse and neglect in detention centres and welfare homes designed to protect them; they are stigmatised and shunned by mainstream society. The World Report on Violence against Children presented to the United Nations in 2006 (14) recognised children who work or live on the streets as being particularly at risk of violence.

Combined and compounded effects of abuse and deprivation undermine their chances of developing into healthy young people and adults. However, each street child has a unique story of violence and a different strategy and ability to cope with it, often with surprising resilience. Gender, age, ethnicity and disability influence the risks of violence to which they are exposed and their response. For example, street boys tend more to replicate violence as aggressors and report more physical violence while girls tend to internalise violence and may be more vulnerable to on-going abuse and victimisation. Girls also tend to be vulnerable to additional forms of violence in crisis situations when compared with boys and more likely - although by no means exclusively - subjected to sexual violence, often with limited access to preventative measures and health services. Younger children's relative physical weakness can expose them to abuse from older children and adults, although they can also attract protection.

Family relationships form a vital development pathway for children. Domestic violence - whether to a parent or a child - affects each child's development differently, but increases the risk of danger for children in other environments too. Evidence that street children have experienced violence in the home - from active physical, sexual or emotional abuse through to neglect - is overwhelming across the world. However, it is important to understand that socio-economic, cultural and community circumstances can undermine the potential of families to care for children.

In countries as diverse as Bangladesh and the UK, children, service providers and researchers point to family violence as a key factor in pushing children onto the streets. Recent research in Bangladesh (15) found: 'moves to the street are closely associated with violence to, and abuse of, children within the household and local community.' In the UK, family conflict and problems at home were found to be the most common factors leading to an under 16-year-old's decision to run away and/or live on the streets (1). Research in the 1990s in Brazil (16) found that most street living boys left home for street life because of changes in family structure within the context of poverty and a wider culture accepting of violent child-rearing practices. Sexual abuse, violence and emotional neglect exist at all levels of society, but children who live in material deprivation and in fragmented communities may feel that they have nowhere to turn but to the street.

Poor neighbourhoods tend to have weak infrastructure with fewer linkages between community based organisations such as schools, health centres, day-care options and grass-roots organisations. Street children are commonly excluded from schools as a result of fights, aggressive reaction to teachers, or threats of violence to other children, or withdrawn by families unable to pay school fees, buy uniforms or school materials. Truancy is also common by children who feel intimidated, unable to keep up or feel misunderstood. Children who experience violence at home and are excluded from school are cut off from a potentially important source of neighbourhood connection and support. The use of corporal punishment in schools humiliates children while reinforcing the cultural acceptance of violence as a form of control.

Violence against children in the street plays out in public places and so receives more attention than the many other environments in which street children experience abuse. Much of this violence is attributed to police, although abuse also comes from other street inhabitants - older youths and adults and from members of the public who may feel harassed by, or contemptuous of, street children. Public hostility and stigmatisation on the basis of their appearance and activities are a common form of violence - revealed in the local words used to label street children. In Rwanda the term 'Mayibobos' harbours connotations of 'filth' and 'criminality'; in Egypt a street-living child is a 'Sewas', an Arabic word for a small insect which destroys crops; 'Throwaways' is a common term in the USA for child runaways; 'Chokara' meaning 'scavenger' in Kenya; 'Borco' in Ethiopia is an adulteration of the Italian words 'sporco' meaning 'filthy' and 'porco' meaning 'pig'. In December 2006, Egyptian society was shocked out of complacency: a 26 year-old man, known as 'El Torbino', made headlines after his arrest for raping and murdering more than thirty street children, throwing them off the top of the 'Torbini' Cairo-Alexandria express train.

Street children - because of neglect or rejection by others - get involved with street and criminal gangs and drug use, initially using intoxicating inhalants and often leading onto hard drugs with an escalation in violence to obtain the drugs and police action; this often fails to discriminate between the criminal gang leaders and children who hang around the same environments.

There have been many reports across the world of police violence against street children in public places. Periodic round-ups, extortion, threats, physical abuse, victimisation, rape and murder by police officers have been documented time and again by street children, service providers, the media, lawyers and researchers. Police violence is sometimes associated with a street-sweeping campaign in anticipation of some major high profile world political or sporting event. Possibly the most notorious police atrocity against street children was what became known as the Candelaria Massacre in Rio de Janeiro, when six street children were murdered by gunfire on 25th July 1993 as they slept on the steps of the Candelaria Church. Three years later a member of the Brazilian Military Police was convicted for his part in the massacre. Another rare victory for street children in the battle against violence was an Inter-American Court on Human Rights ruling in 2001, which ordered the State of Guatemala to pay more than half a million dollars to the families of five street children who were brutally tortured and murdered by two National Policemen in 1990. Such police violence may be state-sponsored or attributed to 'rogue elements' in the police force who sometimes join community vigilante groups formed by local business or community interests to rid themselves of those they consider undesirable or a threat to the appearance of their businesses or neighbourhoods.

Children are regularly subjected to violence by gangs of older street children who exercise fierce control over available informal work. A 13 year-old boy in Nigeria reported being unable to find work in the local market without paying a bribe to older boys. Unable to earn and therefore eat, younger boys would try to sneak into the market but would get a serious beating if they were caught. Many gangs of older street youth control rigidly various income raising activities - at some railway stations in India different gangs control the scavenging of recyclable materials from specific groups of platforms and children attempting to infiltrate these will be warned off with threats of violence. In Harare, Zimbabwe, street children live in gangs and sleep in one place they call their 'base'. This base is fiercely protected from outsiders including other street children. Each gang has a leader who is feared and respected by other gang members - he is usually the best fighter and may have a violent character. Drug use is regularly reported as a source of violent flare-ups between street children in many countries.

Street children are often removed from the street or encouraged to leave public spaces ostensibly for 'reform', 'rehabilitation', or 'protection'. But their reports of abuse and neglect in detention centres and welfare shelters are received from countries across the world. Research with runaways on the railway platforms of Moscow's largest termini (10) suggests that a high proportion are running away from state run orphanages and a substantial number of the 100,000 under 16-year-old runaways reported in the UK every year are running from children's homes (4) . Accounts of violence against street children are commonly recorded in juvenile detention centres and adult prisons. Physical, sexual and psychological abuses are perpetrated by guards, adult detainees and other child detainees. Violence in government institutions reflects, at best, continuing stigmatisation and neglect of street children and, at worst, state encouragement of violence against children. This normalises violence for street children and can exacerbate the effects of previous violence, whether as victims or perpetrators. Even NGO shelters and other residential services for street children can perpetuate abuse, if only by concentrating children accustomed to violence in overcrowded, poorly conditioned, under-managed and under-staffed conditions. Child protection systems are in force for many NGOs but on their own they are not enough if supervision is flimsy or unregulated.

When social institutions are stressed and community cohesion breaks down in times of war, natural disasters, health epidemics or rapid urbanisation, children's risk of violence grows as protective barriers crumble. Violence at large is reflected especially in the situation for children, many being forced on to the streets as a result of reduced protection and collapse of normal family environments. Once on the streets they may be faced by higher levels of violence where the capacity of protection systems has broken down or become swamped by the large number of children at risk.

The children's voices:

*Tyler has never met his father as he left before Tyler's birth and didn't leave a forwarding address. His mother struggled to provide financially and was often unhappy; Tyler has early memories of his mother crying and spending a lot of time in bed. Tyler did his best to comfort her and make her laugh. When Tyler was six, his mother met a man and the close relationship previously shared with his mother changed and Tyler felt rejected. Tyler's stepfather treated him with indifference at best and with violence when he was drunk. He was also violent to Tyler's mother. Tyler hated to see his mother being hurt and tried to defend her, only to be met with more violence. Tyler asked his mother to tell his stepfather to go but his mother said she couldn't do that and seemed resigned to accepting that both Tyler and her were harmed by her partner.*

*Tyler began to stay out on the streets after school to avoid going home. He got to know a group of young males older than him who invited him to join their gang. At eleven, Tyler was introduced to cannabis and petty crime and started to stay out all night. He began to miss school and was excluded for the first time when he was twelve. By the time he was thirteen he had left school completely. Whilst Tyler enjoyed being with his friends, he often felt sad and lonely. His mother's depression worsened and she spent most of her time in bed. After an argument with his stepfather that turned into a fight, Tyler's stepfather told Tyler's mother to choose: either Tyler went or he would leave. Tyler's mother said she couldn't make that choice and Tyler left.*

At first he stayed with different friends, stealing to survive and spending the odd night out of the streets when there was no offer of a bed. He started to drink alcohol regularly and became aggressive when he was drunk. By the time he was fifteen, the offers of a place to sleep became less frequent and Tyler spent more time on the streets, becoming a familiar face on the homeless scene. Sometimes Tyler gets into fights and has been beaten up a number of times. Tyler knows he has a problem with alcohol and anger but doesn't want to access any of the support available to him, preferring to keep his problems to himself. Tyler hasn't seen his mother for over a year and has started to view his homeless friends as family and the streets as home. Tyler doesn't plan for the future but takes each day as it comes; of which some are harder than others. If he gets a drink, has enough food to eat and stays out of the way of the police, that's a good day.

**Tyler, England - Railway Children**

The nine year old boy was trafficked from another State by a middle class man who was unmarried at the time. He did send the child to school. The project had undertaken a huge school awareness programme on child labour and the teachers were worried about the boy's situation. Then the man married and the situation went downhill fast - the boy was tortured and beaten with iron rods and wire. He was rescued by the police and placed in the project's half-way house. He had to be hospitalised to treat his wounds, but managed to go back to school after he'd recovered. He's now doing well and the school are waiving his fees.

**Young boy, Darjeeling - Edith Wilkins Street Children Foundation**

'He used to beat me and he tried to stab me… It was over a bean sandwich…Just the tiniest wee things used to set him off; so it did. Even if I went to the toilet, he used to crack up with me … He wrapped the telephone chord around my neck, pulled it so hard he thought I wasn't breathing and put me in a cold bath so I'd start breathing again… And my daddy broke two of my fingers; he tried to boot my face and I put up my hands to protect my face and he kicked my fingers and broke them… I had a cat and I really loved my cat and he used to make me choose between me getting it or the cat and I always used to say me 'cos I couldn't bear my cat getting hurt…'

**12 year old girl, Scotland - Railway Children**

'The public does not like to see us. They inform the police to take us away…'

**Street Boy, Ethiopia – Retrak**

'Sometimes I felt rejected by other people, they don't want to be close to me because they thought I would hurt them, because they think that all people that work on the street steal, murder and smoke drugs.'
**Street Boy, Ecuador – Juconi**

'One or two people would treat you badly. They'd say things like 'go away'. They would say lots of things, but I don't want to say what they said. It makes me feel bad because they don't know how you feel and they don't care either.'
**Street Girl, Ecuador – Juconi**

'I realised that my father didn't love my mother. Sometimes he would bring my mother some money for food and other times he didn't, but demanded food from my mother. If there was no food, he starts beating her, something which I didn't like and, you see, I wasn't able to change anything because… I was still young and wasn't able to do anything apart from just watching.'
**Matatzio, East Africa – Railway Children**

'I didn't like the idea of making me repeat class at school… The teachers love you if your mother gives them something… If there was noise in the class, the monitor wrote down the names; he'd write mine down and then I'd get beaten. I'd go home and tell my mother what happened and then she'd beat me again. … I've been beaten before now by every teacher in the school. Sometimes I'd hang out in the market with other boys. One morning my mum stopped me and asked me how many days it was since I'd been to school. I told her about a week. So the teachers beat me, all of them together with my mother…in front of the other students. They grabbed me, put my head inside my desk someone's holding me, then they beat me..;. every teacher ten times – there were eight of them. I've not been back to school or home since…'

'I was someone who had the job of carrying parcels. Because other boys saw I was a clean person, they said 'he's not a street child.' When I got money I was robbed just like that by these boys…'
**Samuel, East Africa – Railway Children**

'When I entered the street here, I met some other youths who had been used to street life so they asked me where I was sleeping… They took my shoes by force, beat me up. They told me to move away from the place

*where I slept. Sometimes you get hit with a rock... It was like that until I was getting used to street life, so nobody could easily chase me away.'*
**Ouga, East Africa – Railway Children**

*Whilst participating in the 'Struggling to Survive' research, the children and youths presented a range of injuries such as a nostril slashed with a knife by a friend, a foot sole cut in retaliation for an unpaid fine of 2,000 Tanzanian shillings, and damaged eyes from being beaten by police with a stick. One boy said, 'You may be sleeping and someone can come and set you on fire at night, they set your feet on fire. There was one boy who was killed sometimes back...he was hit by his friend with a stone and he died.'*
**Street Children, East Africa – Railway Children**

**In view of the fact that so many street children experience violence, it is a tribute to many of them that they frequently cope with their situation and even show remarkable resilience. Low self-esteem, depression and self-hatred has been found to be characteristics of street-homeless children in some settings, but many children cope in dangerous street conditions and some show well-developed abilities to navigate street risks. A child who copes with violence by running away may be more resilient than the sibling who stays at home, if the flight denotes a healthy response in being unwilling to be a passive victim.**

# Chapter 4
## *Abuse, Exploitation and Corruption*

UN Convention on the Rights of the Child:

Article 34: 'State Parties undertake to protect the child from all forms of sexual exploitation and sexual abuse.'

Article 35: 'State Parties shall take all appropriate national, bilateral and multilateral measures to prevent the abduction of, sale of or traffic in children for any purpose or in any form.'

Article 36: 'State Parties shall protect the child against all other forms of exploitation prejudicial to any aspects of the child's welfare.'

**Photograph courtesy of Railway Children**

Many children who finish up living a large part of their childhood on the street suffer abuse, both as a push factor causing the child to run from home in the first place, or during the weeks and years they spend on the street. This abuse can take a number of forms - the most common form expressed by the children will be that of physical abuse - beatings at home, corporal punishment at school, bullying by peers. A substantial number of children report being the victims of sexual abuse, usually from people known to them rather than from strangers. Even more children will have suffered from emotional abuse and neglect, but this is difficult to substantiate as few children report this and statistics are rarely available. The public, through the media, have become more aware in the last decade of the scale of sexual and physical abuse of children in general - the World Health Organisation was quoted in the United Nations General Secretary's Report on Children and Violence (2006) (14) as claiming that 150 million girls and 73 million boys under the age of 18 had experienced forced sexual intercourse or sexual violence involving physical contact during the year 2002. Even in high/middle income countries, this same report stated that 7% of girls and 3% of boys had been victims of sexual abuse during their childhood. The UN report identifies street children as one of the groups of children that are particularly vulnerable to physical and sexual abuse.

The Indian government published a 200+ page report entitled 'A study on Child Abuse - India 2007' researched by Save the Children , UNICEF and a Delhi based NGO, Prayas, which documented the results of 12,447 interviews with children, of whom 18.6% were street children (55% boys, 45% girls) (17). A further 8% of children interviewed were children in institutions - government remand homes, children's homes and privately run shelter homes. Another 20% were classified as working children, many of whose work would be street based. This report seems to be the most comprehensive one undertaken on the issue of child abuse by any national government and use is made in this chapter of its findings on street children as an indicator of the likely scale of abuse suffered by street children worldwide.

The World Health Organisation defines physical abuse as 'an incident resulting in actual or potential physical harm from an interaction or lack of interaction, which is reasonably within the control of a parent or person in a position of responsibility, power or trust.' In the Indian study, the forms of physical abuse are described as 'kicking, slapping, corporal punishment, beating by the family, peers, police, employer or care-giver.' In many cultures, children are seen as the 'possessions' of their parents who have total power over them, and in such cultures there seems to have been little resistance by children as the violence has become normalised in their experience. The most common reaction when children can take no more has been to run away. Domestic violence, corporal punishment in schools, bullying by peers is thus one of the major 'push factors' resulting in street children with little family contact. In the Indian study over three quarters (77%) of all children interviewed reported having received physical abuse at some stage in their lives and for many it was ongoing. In 15% of cases the abuse had led to injury.

The experience of violence to children on the street was described in more detail in the previous chapter. Suffice to say that 69% of Indian street children interviewed reported being on the receiving end of violence on the street, with children aged 5-12 reporting most. This figure rose to over 90% in certain parts of India, Delhi itself being the worst followed by the populous and poor states of Uttar Pradesh and Rajasthan.

Street children report sexual abuse as a common feature in their lives. Young street boys and girls often experience sexual advances from older street children and it becomes a normal activity among gangs of children left without adult supervision or care. It becomes one of the few ways in which the children experience affection and the resultant trauma can be reduced as the child may not see the experience as abuse. The children in such situations may have little choice, however, and for some girls seeking a 'protector' from the male street gang may be the only way she can survive. For many children the sexual abuse is more violent involving rape, perpetrated by older street youths, young criminal adults, the police or members of the public, often when inebriated, who see the street children as a sub-human species. The Indian study classified their interview results in two ways on this subject. 'Severe' abuse included rape, sodomy, physical fondling, forced nudity and being photographed in a sexual act for pornographic purposes. 'Other' forms of sexual abuse were forced kissing, sexual verbal advances or teasing, sexual exhibitionism and exposing a child to pornography. Over 21% of the children in the Indian study had experienced 'severe' sexual abuse - 40% of these before the age of 12, and a further 25% at the ages of 13 and 14. The study does not break down the percentage of street children within these figures but states that the children reporting the highest amounts of severe sexual abuse were street children, working children (especially girl domestic servants) and children in institutions.

A further risk to street children and children in slum areas spending time on the street rather than school is that of being trafficked. Parents of girls in particular are offered supposed opportunities to earn good money or are even given down payments, for the child to find herself either in unpaid domestic service or the sex trade. All too often the traffickers have bribed their way to ensure their protection and it is often hard to distinguish between children being trafficked and families travelling with children. A couple of Indian NGOs (18) have expressed the same worrying statement that it is difficult to find girls above the age of ten living on the street or railway station environs although plenty under that age can be seen. The implications they draw are ominous. Children rescued from trafficking face a further challenge when being taken home. Their families or communities often reject such children as being stigmatised with the shame of having been sexually used and therefore unmarriageable.

Many street children are corrupted by their experiences on the street. Because there are so few legitimate ways of surviving without education or adult skills, street children are quickly forced to employ means of existence that are rejected or condemned by society. Desperation and hunger may force children to beg and steal. They become enticed into gangs carrying out illegal activities, and their moral senses become dulled through the sheer necessities of their daily life. Once they have been introduced to intoxicants, either alcohol or inhalants or both, their corruption is intensified and the structure of their lives unravels. In parts of Latin America, young children in the favelas are attracted to the gangs, as they are one of the few parts of society that offer such children 'respect' and status, and then become victims in the warfare between police and criminal gangs even though they may only be existing on the periphery. The longer a child stays on the street, the more will the corruption of that child be embedded and the harder it will be for the child to be rehabilitated in a structured and positive way.

The abuse of children continues unfortunately in the very institutions that are meant to be protecting such children. Street children or children at risk of taking to the street are often found 'in need of care and protection' and taken into a children's residential home of some sort 'in their best interests'. In India, children picked up by the police and produced before city or state Child Welfare Committees are usually placed in what is called an 'Observation Home' where a mixture of children accused of petty crimes and innocent homeless children are put together, although steps are now being taken in conjunction with NGOs to monitor the observation of the rights and welfare of children in these institutions. In Russia, children of alcoholics, drug addicts and parents in prison are classified as 'social orphans' their parents being deprived of their parental rights, and the children placed in one of the state orphanages. In many of these conditions are so poor that the children run to the streets as a preferable option. A study at the railway stations of Moscow found that nearly 50% of runaways interviewed had run from state orphanages (10). In the UK in the last couple of decades there have been a number of scandals alleging child abuse in children's homes and many of the 100,000 annual reported runaways are children absconding from such institutions (1). It is only in the last few years that steps have been taken in many countries to institute child protection safeguards, vetting the staff employed in activities involving children and requiring strict child safeguarding practices.

The consequences of ignoring the abuse of so many children is that society and the children become hardened to such abuse and see it as a norm for their own behaviours. Young street children, abused by older children, may become abusers in turn when they are in positions of power in the hierarchy unless they have been sensitised to the needs of others by someone who shows care for them. Many adults accused of criminal violence or sexual acts against children claim to have been abused as children themselves. A research study on 'detached' children in the UK identifies that most of the hundred children researched in depth had parents who themselves had led abused lives (1).

*On a freezing winter's night in a famous tourist town in England, Charlene, aged thirteen, is spending the night under a railway arch with a group of homeless adults. Charlene's father started to sexually abuse*

31

Charlene when she was nine and, by the time she was eleven, repeatedly raped her. Her father drank too much and bullied her mother who was depressed and spent a lot of time in bed. When Charlene was twelve, she could no longer cope with what her father was doing to her and ran away, preferring to be on the streets than in a home where she lived in dread of a father who would not report her missing because of what he had been doing and a mother who won't protect her because she fears her husband. Charlene's family now is a group of homeless adults, some of whom remind her that the streets are dangerous for a young girl. At the mention of social services, Charlene threatens to run from her street family; from her perspective, social services failed to protect her when she was living at home and being abused. While Charlene, now thirteen, describes how some of her street family look out for her, protect her and share what little they have with her, others encourage her to take heroin and one homeless adult has become her boyfriend.

**Charlene, England - Railway Children**

Abuse is a serious issue for many street and high risk children – whether it is physical, mental or sexual. At the age of eight, Madeline, became a domestic servant. She tells her story below.

'My Mum met a family in Lima. They wanted me to work for them. They promised to send me to school... I didn't want to go, but Mum said I would have a better life. The first few months everything was fine. But then the man changed. He used to look at me strangely, making gestures I didn't like. I was afraid... I told the man's wife but she said I was a liar... I felt bad and guilty...'

It wasn't long before the abuse began. Fortunately Madeline's school teachers noticed something was wrong. Madeline wasn't paying attention in class and seemed depressed. Eventually Madeline opened up to a teacher who helped her escape and report the abuse.

Madeline is now 16 years old and living safely in a home supported by British NGO, Toybox. At the home, Madeline and 15 other abused girls receive care, education and psychological support. They can stay in safety for as long as they need. Madeline's house parents are doing everything possible to find her family. In the meantime, Madeline is carrying on with her life and has new hope for the future:

'I have found people who love me very much and are helping me to overcome my pain. One day I would like to be a teacher to help other children.'

**Madeline, Lima - Toybox**

'I was born on Christmas Eve. When I was five, my mother gave me to a lady because she didn't want me anymore. The lady made me beg on the streets for money. When I was nine, I was forced to have sex with many men. If I refused I would be burned with lighted cigarettes. I have many scars now because of this.

Then I was given away to another family, who would beat me all the time. The man in the family raped me and I got pregnant. When the baby was born, they took it off me and I ran away to live on the streets. Because of these experiences I grew up with a hatred in my heart against all men who tried to become 'my friend'. I am ashamed to say that I became a lesbian, because women aren't as bad as men and my girlfriend made me feel safe and secure. That was two years ago, before I met a group of Christians who told me about God and gave me somewhere to live. I knew I needed to change. I didn't want to keep living like that. I was tired and - most of all – I was hurting God. I want to change and live for Jesus. Now I have a home and a future.'

Marleny enjoyed another three years in the home before she left and began living with an older lady and got a job selling food on a street corner. Sadly, she did not finish her studies and went back to her old ways for a while. When last heard of, she was doing much better but still very mixed up and seeking affirmation.

**Marleny, Guatemala – Street Kids Direct**


*According to press reports, 500 displaced Nepalese children were living in Indian children's homes in conditions that only met the most basic needs. The Esther Benjamin Trust which works in Nepal researched why these children were there and concluded that many had been trafficked and 'rescued' into these so-called child-care centres. A visit made to a Delhi home uncovered six Nepali children and the NGO managed to trace their families in Nepal. News of the children's whereabouts was greeted with both elation and suspicion. The uncle of one of the boys told of rumours that the children had been kidnapped and burnt alive. Three boys were collected from one home, but difficulties arose where the other boys were rumoured to be. The home was protected with patrol guards and high walls and barbed wire. Entry was denied to the boys' parents until a local Indian NGO interceded for them. After battling with seemingly insurmountable obstacles, the case went to Court and with the help of Childline India and invoking the provisions of the Indian Juvenile Justice Act, five of the children were released back to their families. The sixth, said to have run away, was listed as still 'missing'.*

**Esther Benjamin Trust, Nepal**

Sumitra is now fourteen years old and has just enrolled in Class 2 in a local school after having stayed in the Shakti Samuha shelter for two months. This is a remarkable achievement considering her story. Sumitra does not have a father at home – he left when she was young. From the age of eleven Sumitra was sent to beg on the street by her mother who realised that her daughter would earn more money begging than she would. This pushed Sumitra into a street environment where she began to make friends while earning money for her family. When she had reached twelve years of age her uncle began to repeatedly sexually abuse her and other girls of her age in their extended family. While it appears that her mother and others in the family knew of this, the uncle was never challenged nor was it spoken about. Sumitra became accustomed to the street and having faced the experience of abuse and with a degraded sense of self-worth began to drift towards the city centre where 'massage parlours' and street prostitution are rife. She was aware of the prospects of the money she could earn for what had become normal for her at home in the past year. She spent a few months in this area with taxi drivers and street youth as her clients – often exchanging sex for food. She was not the only one in this situation and even herself brought her younger cousins to the street where their daily abuse became normalised; nor was it questioned or challenged by the local community. The girls themselves would even joke with each other about who had sold themselves for the least remuneration.

An organisation in Kathmandu encountered her and her friends on the street and after building basic relations with the girls decided to support them to move on from the street – this organisation as a rule only worked with boys but made an exception considering their situation. After taking the girls in, Just-One looked for referral centres for the girls but none were willing to take them on – the girls were either 'too challenging' or organisations did not believe the girls could or would change. Through Kidasha, Sumitra was referred to our local partner, Shakti Samuha, with another three friends of a younger age from the same situation as her. While one girl has returned to the street two other girls have been referred for residential counselling and support in a local counselling centre in Pokhara – this is where Sumitra was initially referred but she was 'returned' by the centre staff who said they were unable to deal with her.

While there remain many challenges, Sumitra has found a family and an environment in Shakti Samuha for her to recover among many other girls who have faced similar experiences. Her confidence and self-esteem have increased and her enrolment in school is a big step for her back into

34

*mainstream society. Soon her two friends will return to Shakti Samuha and it is hoped they will follow in her footsteps. The long-term future for these girls is more challenging: as more than thirty days had passed since sexual abuse at the hands of the uncle, a case could not be registered against him. In addition none of the family members were willing to challenge the uncle. The girls cannot return home to an abusive situation and one where they are neglected and most likely to return to the street. Over time Shakti Samuha will work with the girls to find alternative solutions – the younger ones may be able to adapt to life in a children's home but for Sumitra she is too old to be accepted. Adapting to mainstream society and having the strength to take on life independently will be a tough challenge for Sumitra but at least now she knows she has a family that cares for her. Shakti Samuha and her new sisters will work in whatever way they can to support her through the challenges that she will have to face in the coming years.*

**Sumitra, Nepal – Kidasha**

*The girl had been raped several times on the station and had been through a programme of counselling with professionals from the project. However, she found it difficult to get into or keep a normal relationship. She met a guy who promised to marry her, but when it came to it, he ended up abusing her. After 14 hours of torture she was rescued. Her lips had had cigarettes put out on them, similarly her arms and legs. He'd used a hammer on her back and legs and broke a bottle and scarred her face and other parts of her body. She was raped again and again during this torture. The project team got him arrested but when it came to court the girl couldn't face the ordeal. The man was released on bail of 200 rupees (£3) and walked away scot-free. She had a baby as a result of that abuse and is now bringing him up as a single mum. She's had work training but has, understandably, huge problems. However, she adores her little son and is doing great as a mum with much support.*

**Girl, Darjeeling - Edith Wilkins Street Children Foundation**

*Thirty young girls were found living on the railway platform of Howrah, Calcutta, in 1998. The youngest was four, the oldest thirteen. All had been raped or sexually abused, several were HIV+. One of the girls aged twelve was already a prostitute – when she told the older girls she'd been raped, they suggested she insisted on payment. One of the younger girls, 'B', a seven year old, survived by carrying water for eight hours every day of the year for the local slum community – the nearest source of clean water was a kilometre away. For this she received the*

35

princely sum of a rupee a day (just over a penny) and had to survive on that. A local school loaned their classroom to a Calcutta NGO, SEED, who hired two social workers to act as 'aunties' to the girls. Every evening at six the girls would be met with a wash, clean clothes, a hot meal. Afterwards they received health advice, basic lessons in reading and writing, and entertainment – they loved dancing. They were able to sleep unmolested, some for the first time in their lives, but at 8 o'clock they went back to the street as the school needed its classroom back. Subsequently SEED acquired proper accommodation and its UK partner, Railway Children, received an e-mail from 'B' a couple of years ago 'thanking them for giving her childhood back.'

**Street Girls, Calcutta - Railway Children**


'I guess all I do is do something else that distracts me, but this doesn't solve the problem. Actually problems are never solved.'

**Street Girl, Moroccan Children's Trust**


'I don't tell anyone. For me, I get used to it, whatever troubles me. There is no-one I can really trust so it just stays inside me, even if it gets worse that way.'

**Street Girl, Moroccan Children's Trust**


When Turusifu was aged ten, two older boys raped him while he was trying to sleep. He felt terrible, found a tunnel and slept for two days, only leaving when hunger forced him to do so. A short time later he was given a small amount of money by a kind man. The boys who raped Turusifu saw him being given this money and followed him to the river, where, after buying soap, he was washing his clothes. They raped him again and stole his clothes leaving only his underpants. Turusifu went to the garbage dump to look for clothes and found some trousers and a shirt. 'The two boys came back and tried to force me down to do it again. I refused, I fought back. They took a knife and started stabbing me on my knees.'

**Turusifu, East Africa – Railway Children**


Some of the street boys expressed an acceptance that rape by the older youths on the streets was inevitable; these older youths had been raped when they were younger and they, in turn, raped the younger boys. One boy, during a particularly frank interview, after being asked if he had been raped, shrugged his shoulders and replied that of course he had. Many of the boys do not explicitly consent or welcome the sexual advances of others, but accept that they are powerless to resist older and stronger

36

*males. One of the boys interviewed was Matu, a seven year old tiny child with a big smile who had been gang-raped by boys who had taken him down to the sewers.*

**Matu and other Street Boys, East Africa – Railway Children**

It is shocking that we accept or ignore so much abuse of children around the world, but it is remarkable that despite such experiences, so many children have a resilience that enables them to survive. In some cases it is because of the sheer commonality of the experience - so many children in the community experience the abuse that they accept it as normal and do not see it as abuse at all. This can be the case in countries where school corporal punishment is still the norm and where children might only react when a beating is particularly excessive. Street children living within a gang of other street children quickly find sexual interplay between the children to be the norm and appear to be unfazed by the experience. Most street children are remarkably resilient. They bury their traumas in cheekiness, aggression, fighting and teasing their peers, or, especially in the case of girls, become passive and stoical, withdrawn. To restore such children's self-worth and rehabilitate them so they can take their place in society, hold down a job, and raise a family successfully, requires the dedication of professional counsellors and carers. But society must face this or in every decade the number of damaged children will increase as the failures of one generation are replicated in the next.

# Chapter 5
## *Work* (19)

UN Convention on the Rights of the Child, Article 32: 'State parties recognize the right of the child to be protected from economic exploitation and from performing any work that is likely to be hazardous or to interfere with the child's education, or to be harmful to the child's health or physical, mental, spiritual, moral or social development.'

**Photograph by Marcus Lyon**

The immediate needs of a child thrust into the confusing and dangerous world of an unknown city are for food or money to buy food, for shelter and for affection and the company of others. A child's response is to survive one day at a time, and an obvious way for a child to seek to survive is through trying to find work on the street - casual and informal trade.

Some 5-10% of street children in most cities are abandoned, orphaned or runaway children with, at best, sporadic contact with their families. In fact, for them their families consist of other street children loosely formed in gangs or small groups which demonstrate considerable loyalty to their members. These children sleep where they can - in shop doorways, covered bus and railway stations, under market stalls, in parks and on beaches. Unless such children can find an NGO to provide food and shelter, they will be dependent on their own efforts or those of other street children in their 'family' to find food, or the means to pay for it.

Such children gather round locations where the possibility of casual labour exists. They seek out adults who can provide them with some activity in return for which they receive food and possibly some protection. Such activities include running errands, helping out at street vending, scavenging for refuse that can be sorted and recycled, collecting empty water bottles, refilling and selling. Many of these activities are dangerous, especially for younger children. Most will involve exposure to road accident risks, darting into traffic to ply their trade. Indian street children cluster round railway stations, jumping on and off moving trains or jumping down onto the track to scavenge, acquire seats for passengers, carry luggage and clean train compartments, and many children are injured, some severely or fatally. One Indian NGO in Andhra Pradesh [20], which had a grant specifically allocated for hospital and medical expenses incurred by street children in road and rail accidents, used the fund for 48 children in a twelve month period.

A further risk to these children is that they are dependent on relationships they forge with the adults for whom they operate, and whilst some are sympathetic and protective, many adults exploit the children treating them as cheap labour and expendable, often reacting with violence towards the child if he or she incurs their temporary displeasure. Others - and this will often include older street youth who lead the gangs - will sexually abuse the younger children as part of the price for their protection - survival sex.

If children cannot find any activity that will provide money for food, they scavenge for left-overs in trains, dustbins, around restaurants and market places, risking disease. Children unable to work, through age, disability or sickness, beg or become dependent on an exploitative adult or group of older children. In extremis children get involved in illegal activities in order to survive. If rejected by their peers or other members of society, they turn to activities that put them at greater risk from the authorities. They start by stealing trivial bits of food or money for food. They may get involved with a gang that forces them to steal more systematically. They may get involved with errands for drug dealers and / or in commercial sex. Interviews with 1,000 street children by a Mumbai based NGO (7) in 1993 found children had a strong sense of hierarchy of activities ranged by desirability, and would resort to begging, stealing, drug activities and sex-selling in that order - and only if they could survive in no other way.

These children, especially those without some protective structure, are at constant risk of losing whatever cash or food they've managed to acquire, so this breeds a culture that does not look beyond the immediate present. If a child has money left over after buying immediate food needs, he or she will spend it on some cheap entertainment or even gamble it away. A nine year old on Ahmedabad station in India, when asked how he stopped older boys stealing his money, said *I buy food and eat it straight away - they can't steal it from my belly.* (21)  Many children who have acquired money through illicit activities will find they have to pay protection money or provide sex in lieu of cash to police or criminal gangs, who would otherwise arrest them or beat them up.

Children of street living families and slum children are heavily involved in activities such as scavenging for refuse that is capable of being sold for recycling. Rag-picking is a variation of this activity that occupies many young children. The environment of such activity is particularly dangerous for children - the filth and open sewers, plus the dangers from infected items discarded expose these children to diseases, both chronic and acute. In some slum areas children are removed from schools to provide income for families where no breadwinner exists or the adults are unemployed or sick. Children are employed in small factories, tea stalls, petty vending activities, often for excessively long hours and for a pittance. The margin between classifying such children as child labourers and street children is ill defined, for such children will spend time on the streets seeking to augment the family income further in addition to any informal employment off the street.

Such children are frequently abused both sexually and physically as a result of failure to meet the performance required by their taskmasters. Street living children often cite a beating by someone for whom they worked as the catalyst for their leaving home. Others blame violence from a father or stepfather when they fail to make enough money from their activities as a cause of their running away. Children on the street are rarely supervised and are open to pressures detrimental to both their health and morals. Seen as a nuisance at best by much of society, their self-worth perception is low and they can be easy prey for unscrupulous adults who both exploit and often criminalise them. Their parents can be easily seduced into allowing them to be taken to alleged jobs in hotels, restaurants, bars and private domestic work, whereas in reality they are introduced into the commercial sex trade or trafficked to other cities.

Children and youths who commute into city centres from slum suburbs to work undertake a wide variety of jobs of an informal and unregulated nature - shoe-shining, vending activities, collecting and reselling bottles and recyclable materials, windscreen-washing, cleaning, hotel and restaurant casual labour. Many of these activities are 'part-time' leaving the children free to roam the streets and join with other street children. Some of the older children form their own territories and trades which they regulate carefully to avoid newer children competing. Often an adult criminal or gang leader will regulate the activities of such children and youths. Such children can earn sufficient income to spend on entertainment in addition to necessities, but they are operating at the margins of legality and under constant threat from adult operators and the police. In a situational analysis undertaken by 'Railway Children' at New Delhi railway station, many children were found to be earning an average of 180-250 rupees a day, a sum greater than that of many of the voluntary sector workers seeking to help them. However, the children complained bitterly of police and gangster violence and the lack of facilities to help them escape from drug and alcohol addiction to which they had been exposed.

Because the public's perception of street children is negative - they are seen as dirty, delinquent, at best a nuisance, at worst a danger especially when in a gang of other street children - the children are at risk of abuse by those in authority who should be protecting them. The children are often rounded up by the police under laws against vagrancy or loitering. They are arrested on suspicion of committing petty crimes. Those children who are thought to have cash from their various trading and other earning opportunities are open to protection rackets from adult criminals, street gang leaders and to police corruption, with threats of violence if they resist. Therefore these children have little opportunity to save money and find ways of bettering themselves and developing legitimate ways of getting themselves off the street in the longer term.

The experiences of the children:

*I encountered a six year old street girl on Churchgate railway station, Mumbai. She was lashing her back with a home-made whip to provoke sympathy from gullible tourists like me and entice me to give generously money which I realised would go straight to the pockets of the unscrupulous adult running her. This was, for this girl, her work. This scene was the catalyst for my involvement with children's rights and, in particular, with organisations campaigning for the millions of exploited, abused and corrupted street children found in virtually every continent.*
**David Maidment – Railway Children**

*Peter is 16 years old and lives alone in a shack in Uganda. He has been a double orphan since the age of 13. He works as a charcoal carrier on the lake shore in order to survive. One bag of charcoal weighs approximately 12 kg and has to be carried roughly 500 metres, struggling through deep shingle, negotiating the hazards and bustle of the lake shores, to reach the warehouses above the port. For each bag carried, Peter gets paid 1,000 Ugandan shillings - just 30 pence. It is unbearably hard physical labour for a young boy, still grieving for his parents, completely alone in the world. Through remarkable tenacity Peter pays his own school fees and rent, and even scrounges scraps for two small pigs he keeps. He is a determined young man who makes difficult choices. He chooses to do a backbreaking job in order to survive. He chooses to pay his fees and go to school because he hopes that education will lead him out of poverty. He chooses to survive.*

*A British NGO worker met Peter during a trip to Uganda. He had severely injured a muscle in his back through carrying too heavy a load. He could hardly breathe from the pain. Unable to work, he now faces the prospect of not being able to pay the rent for his tiny shack and being evicted. School fees will not be possible. He will become a full time street child. Suddenly, at the turn of one small event, Peter has no choices. No money means no home or school, no food or water and in the end, no option for survival. We should be under no illusions; street children who find themselves with no options can and do die. Funeral costs are a common place request when partner NGOs apply for grants.*

**Peter, Jinja, Uganda – Street Child Africa**


*In Rwanda boys and girls leave home at different times. Boys tend to be quicker separating from their families than girls. They have options; they can potentially find work in the market place or carrying goods for shopkeepers. They will have friends already living on the streets encouraging them to join. Girls don't have these 'opportunities', so they wait it out a bit longer at home before finding work as house-girls (everyone in Rwanda has a house-girl). In return for working practically as a slave to her new family, the girl will be rewarded with a place to sleep and a few scraps from the family supper. She's unlikely to be paid cash. In too many cases the girl will be subject to sexual abuse, often full rape, by the man of the house. He won't use protection and he may well be HIV+. Soon the girl will be pregnant at which point she is kicked out of the house, unable to go home. She is then forced into prostitution to support herself and her new baby.*

*Not only does she have little education, less chance of getting one, she also has a child, no home, potentially an STI or two. She is universally reviled by the community that tacitly condones the behaviour of the man who put her in this situation. She has no idea how to look after herself adequately, let alone bring up a child. A generation of children born on the street knows nothing different.*

**World Jewish Relief, Rwanda**


*'I started working when I was 5 years old and it was really difficult. I didn't know how to sell anything but I had to stay positive whether I managed to sell anything or not because I knew I would have to go out the next day to sell again. But after a little I learned a bit more about being on the street and I made some friends and they taught me how to sell and*

*stuck with me. I wanted to be in school and be with my family, but we needed help financially but if you didn't work, things aren't just going to fall out of the sky to feed you. I continue to do it because I now like it and not just because we need the money. It's something that I learned to do ...'*
**Street Boy, Ecuador - Juconi**

*'Life is hard. I must sweat to survive.'*
**Street Boy, East Africa – Railway Children**

*The supervisors for the bus stand came to think that if you want to be there to carry luggage, you have to pay. They wanted money. It became so hard I went back with my sack collecting litter... I went back and they agreed I could register at the bus stand for 350 Kenyan shillings (just under £3). Then you had to pay 500 for the uniform... And then they started to say they didn't want someone who slept on the street because they could run away with the passengers' bags.'*
**Chitundu, Nairobi – Railway Children**

**Banning all child labour could in the short to medium term have a detrimental effect on street children, as alternative survival strategies may be far worse - begging, crime, sex-selling. Older street children need emotional support in caring environments and training to turn their entrepreneurial skills to flourish in legitimate areas. They need encouragement to plan for their lives and opportunities to save their earned money safely through such initiatives as the children's bank movement. A priority for these children is the banning of activities which are most harmful and exploitative for children - and the vigorous implementation of such bans - and the protection of the children from those who force them to work excessive hours, deny their rights, or steal their meagre earnings.**

# Chapter 6
## *Health*

UN Convention on the Rights of the Child:
Article 24: 'State Parties recognize the right of the child to the enjoyment of the highest attainable standard of health and to facilities for the treatment of illness and rehabilitation of health ...'
Article 33: 'State Parties shall take all appropriate measures, including legislative, administrative, social and educational measures, to protect children from the illicit use of narcotic drugs and psychotropic substances as defined in the relevant international treaties, and to prevent the use of children in the illicit production and trafficking of such substances.'

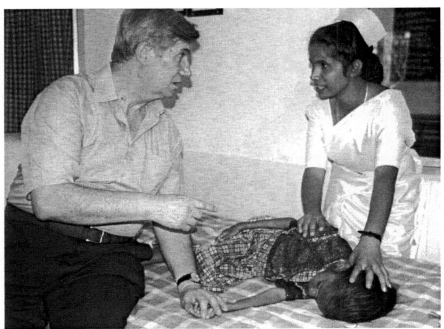

**Photograph courtesy of Railway Children**

It may seem fairly obvious why street children are vulnerable to poor health. If they live in slums, all too often they have to cope with lack of clean water, open sewers, lack of hygienic toilet facilities, lack of waste disposal services, pollution. For lone street children, detached from their families and communities, care for their own health seems to come low in their priorities. These children live one day at a time. Their obsession is to get food or money and to survive the day. They rarely think of the long term, which for many of the children is the next day or next week. If getting food means rummaging through a restaurant's or hotel's waste bins, they will do that. There is no such thing for them as a 'sell-by date'. Often their greatest chance of a drink is the water left at the bottom of a discarded water bottle; or from a street stand-pump; or from the waterpipes that supply a railway carriage or bus cleaning plant. Or rainwater accumulating in filthy puddles.

Few of these children have access to adult health care. A survey conducted in Mumbai several years ago (7) of over a thousand street children found that less than 5% knew how to get adult help. Half of the children looked to another street child for help when they were ill or injured, the rest just put up with, or tried to ignore their problem and let nature take its course. All too frequent an allegation was the impossibility of a street child being accepted for treatment in a hospital unless accompanied by an adult who would be accountable for any costs incurred. Most hospitals in the world - even if purportedly free - still require costs for food and medicines or for adults to supply these to the hospitalised person. Many sick street children report being chased away from hospital entrances unless they are obviously severely injured.

Those NGOs that have facilities for treating sick street children report a multitude of common ailments to which the children are prone. Because of lack of hygiene, sores and skin diseases are common. Bruises and infections from wounds caused in fights and beatings, chest infections from exposure to dampness and pollution, malaria in South Asia and Sub Saharan Africa are rife. You will still find crippled children from the effects of polio or birth abnormalities abandoned on the streets and stations of India begging for a living - partly because their family cannot cope with their upbringing, sometimes because the family has taken advantage of their state to put them to begging for family income.

Throughout Africa, many children are on the street because of the ravages of HIV/AIDS among their parents or extended family of that generation. Older street children themselves fall victim to the same infection through casual and unprotected sex and many street children the world over are vulnerable to HIV because of sexual abuse by infected adults or older street youth. NGOs working with street children find increasing evidence of HIV infected children in Latin America and the Indian sub-continent (22). In Russia and parts of Latin America, infection from the use of shared needles by children who are using hard drugs is becoming very common. It is often difficult to test children to check if they are HIV+ without infringing their rights and with no adults prepared to take legal responsibility for them and therefore it has been hard to produce the necessary evidence to convince major AIDS programmes to treat street children as a priority vulnerable group. NGOs can often only assess the risk and likely prevalence of HIV by noting the extent of sexually transmitted infections that the children display. Most programmes for children are run through schools or communities from which street children by definition are excluded.

One or two NGOs have built hospices for children suffering from AIDS related illnesses - one such in Andhra Pradesh in India (20) , with beds for twenty children, had to admit 26 on the first day it opened. After initial assessment and treatment, the children able to return to the street or their slum families did so; but they had immediate access again if their illness reached a critical or terminal stage. They were not left to die in the gutter which would probably otherwise have been their fate. Attempts to raise awareness of the disease and its risks are often difficult and even taboo subjects in certain cultures. One NGO (23) found its partner organisations' local staff were reluctant to tackle sexual matters openly with the children and found it more effective to train some of the teenage boys who became peer educators. Interestingly, these 14 and 15 year old boys became the 'experts' to the local adult community as well as to other street children and their credibility gave them respect and enhanced their feeling of self-worth.

Accidents among street children are common. In order to gain some advantage over their peers in earning a meagre pittance from some of their activities, they will take risks we would consider unacceptable, rushing into crowded streets, jumping onto or hanging on the outside of moving trains. You will see beggars who have lost a leg or arm in such escapades - often supported by their 'family' or gang of street children. The injured child will often share their takings with the group as they arouse greater sympathy from the occasional passer-by.

Some injuries are less of an accident. In parts of Africa in particular street children are found with injuries deliberately inflicted. In war torn countries, rebel groups and sometimes even government troops recruit children to fight their battles and war wounded children are left on the street when some sort of peace is finally imposed - often rejected by their communities because of atrocities they have been forced to commit - or even suspected of having committed. In Nigeria and parts of the Democratic Republic of Congo many children are accused by their superstitious families of being witches and are deliberately maimed or injured during horrendous forced so-called exorcisms and then rejected by their communities (24). In some countries in Central America there is evidence that street youths have been tortured and murdered by the police or groups of vigilantes - often off-duty police hired by business groups or communities to rid themselves of boys they see as threats (25).

Many of the street children suffer from the self inflicted abuse of drug addiction. Any child who has spent any length of time on the street finds it hard to resist the short term lures of cheap drugs - solvents or other substances that can be inhaled to give a temporary relief from boredom, pain and hunger. A child joining a gang of other children for protection will soon find themselves pressured to join the others in taking some form of drug if only out of camaraderie. And once hooked, they find it difficult to leave. There are very few drug de-addiction facilities that specialise in helping children. The vast majority of such children succumb all too easily to stimulants that they can afford. In Latin America it is 'shoe glue'; in Africa it is glue as well; in India the children find solace in inhaling 'whitener', the fluid still used to correct typing errors and easily available to children in shops that sell simple stationery materials. In Russia, alcohol abuse is just as common as drug abuse. In their drug-intoxicated state street children are even more careless of their health and hygiene practices, and ignore the potential long term harm to escape their present situation through a sought-for continuing 'high'. For older youths with their ability to earn more, all too often they will progress to harder drugs, or become part of a drug distribution criminal network. Drug criminals will use young children to act as 'runners' or distributors' and get the children hooked on drugs so that they find themselves dependent on their abusers.

One enterprising NGO in Delhi (26), whose founder believes strongly in children fighting for their own rights, has formed a 'Health Co-operative'. Over a hundred street children pay a rupee a month to belong and hold their own meetings at which they invite medical experts to come and talk to them about the risks and prevention strategies for various types of illness or injury. This is perhaps the ultimate - and positive - expression of what street children do nearly all the time. That is, to take responsibility for their own health or lack of it.

What is the experience of the children?

*Subu was six years old and was already a street child travelling at will round India's vast railway system. He was with a group of boys hanging out on a long distance train near the city of Visakhapatnam in Andhra Pradesh, when a BBC cameraman came upon him and began to film as the interviewer from Sport Relief began to talk to some of the older boys. The 50 mph train suddenly lurched and young Subu fell from the open door (many Indian trains run with wide-open doors). The film crew pulled the emergency chord and all rushed back expecting to find a corpse – but Subu was still alive though badly injured. After hospitalisation, Subu was taken to Railway Children's partner, which was being filmed for showing in the BBC Telethon later that year, and miraculously, he made a complete recovery.*

**Subu, India – Railway Children**

*Andrew was brought to Retrak from the International Hospital Kampala. A week earlier he had been found lying half dead along Kampala's railway line, a train had run over his left leg and crushed it. The medical staff at the hospital were wondering how this could happen until a peculiar behaviour surfaced - convulsion from fits. It was established that Andrew suffered from epilepsy and must have been crossing the railway when he went into an epileptic attack. He received excellent care, but nevertheless needed to have his left leg amputated. On coming round after his operation he had amnesia and could not believe he had only one leg and found it hard to adjust his movement and* coordination accordingly. It was clear he would need intensive psychological and physical therapy.

With no possible way of identifying his family, or hometown, hospital staff referred Andrew to Retrak where medical staff provided him with counselling, support and a stable loving environment to recuperate. Over time this care enabled him to accept his medical condition, make friends and gain confidence in participating in educational and sporting activities. The Retrak nurse was able to identify a paediatric neurologist who was able to treat Andrew's epilepsy; slowly his fits reduced and became manageable.

Following his excellent physical recovery Andrew eventually remembered his father's name and felt ready to return home to his family. Although he couldn't remember the reason why he had run away, Retrak staff set off to resettle him in his home town near Lugazi. His family explained that he had run away following a family dispute and couldn't believe - having feared the worst - that he had returned home safely. He was so happy, calling out to his siblings saying, 'am back!' Following his traumatic accident on the railway line Andrew is now happily resettled with his extended family and has reintegrated successfully in the local community.

**Andrew, Uganda - Retrak**

*One child described how he was given inadequate medical attention for a deep cut on his head after being in a fight. 'There at the hospital they didn't treat me very well. They just washed me and put on a bandage. They wanted money and I didn't have any.'*
**Street Boy, East Africa – Railway Children**

*'In the beginning I did not believe that the medical check-up, the treatment and the condoms would really be free of charge and anonymous. I thought it was another trap by the police. I agreed to go there with an outreach worker for the first time, but now I go there alone and encourage my friends to use the service as well.'*
**Street Boy, Tajikistan - UN Street Voices Report**

*A Cambodian NGO, M'Lop Tapang, has a drug rehabilitation programme. This starts with offering a safe place for kids to go during the day. This is a separate location from the main street kids' facilities. This allows children to arrive high and to sleep off drugs at anytime of the day. They receive counselling, food, help, medical care and have access to regular exercise and group sports programmes. The on-site, specialised*

52

*staff get to know them closely and visit them on the streets at night. They know their routines, friends, family, drugs of choice. Once a child starts to show signs of tackling their addiction and committing to trying to stop, the programme intensifies. Children and youths are encouraged and if they show a change in attitude after regular visits and counselling sessions, they are then introduced into other M'Lop programmes such as vocational training or education. They continue to be monitored and to work with their original care workers. Relapses happen often and kids disappear often for periods of time. But over the years, the pattern is that they always return and ask for help again. Long-term success rates are high. Programmes have also been set up to help parents of street children – alcohol and drug-addiction support groups.*

### *International Childcare Trust, Cambodia*

*Anderson first came to Viva a Vida in Salvador when he was just 13 years old. He had lived on and off the streets since the age of 8. His mother often went looking for him and brought him home several times, but he never stayed long as he did not get on with his stepfather. On the streets he started glue sniffing and smoking marihuana at an early age. By the time he was 12 he was addicted to crack. He would spend his days begging at traffic lights near a neighbourhood known locally as 'crack-land'. As soon as he made enough money for a crack crystal he would purchase one, smoke it and when the effect wore off, usually after 10 minutes, he would be back at the traffic lights begging in order to buy more.*

*It was his mother who first brought him to Viva a Vida, soon after it opened in 2005. Like others, Anderson struggled to overcome his cravings for crack and went in and out of the programme four times before graduating. The first few times he stayed from 2 weeks to one month, always leaving because he said his drug cravings spoke louder. One particular time, his mother brought in a banjo that he enjoyed playing. The next day he ran away with banjo in tow. To him that banjo ended up representing money for crack. He sold his banjo and bought several crack crystals. As he says 'I smoked up that banjo'. Nevertheless Anderson kept coming back. He always said that he had suffered enough on the streets and did not want to suffer anymore. He participated in individual and group therapy sessions as well as other educational, creative and recreational activities designed to help him build on his strengths and to understand and address his addiction. Anderson went back to school and managed to finish his first year of primary school. At Viva a Vida he also discovered a passion for cooking and now had dreams of becoming a chef. Now at the age of 18, Anderson is drug-free, lives alone in rented*

*accommodation and is doing what he loves: training to be a cook. He still has his difficulties and his moments of self-doubt, as the road to recovery is a long one, but with determination and support he is working towards his dream.*
**Anderson, Salvador, Brazil - Viva a Vida**

*'I felt like my life was in danger but you know once you have sniffed glue you can't even feel anything bigger or serious; instead, you see everything as normal. You just feel like you are on top of everything, you know. I became bold and feared nothing. You don't feel hungry.'*
**Street Boy, East Africa – Railway Children**

*'I get drunk so as not to feel cold at night.'*
**Street Boy, East Africa – Railway Children**

*'I fell sick and that is why I refrained from using. I used to cough seriously in the morning when I woke up and felt pains here (in my chest) and I couldn't run … I was admitted to one of the wards and when I was discharged, they warned me about sniffing gum. From that time, I've never sniffed glue again.'*
**Aluna, East Africa – Railway Children**

*A few years ago a fire broke out in an illegal slum settlement beside the railway line in a Calcutta suburb. The fire, started by an overturned oil stove, spread rapidly through the 200 strong community and devastated the slum - the only building left standing was a simple bamboo school where the local NGO gave informal lessons to the children who spent most of the time on the street. Many people, including children, were badly burned and one child died. No fire engines, no ambulances came, no help, other than the project's visiting Irish and UK trustees. One went with a local doctor and bought all the medicines and first aid equipment they could afford from rapidly pooled cash they all had on them. The trustee from Ireland and the Irish nurse who was advisor to the project applied the best treatment they could give, following diagnosis by the doctor, to the queue of patient stoical men, women and children who had been injured. The other trustee sat on the scorched earth of the little school acting as medical orderly trying to find the right medicines, or cutting plasters and cotton wool, amid the cacophony of Bengali, Hindi and Irish accents. Just as the last patient victim had been treated, after some 4-5 hours of toil, a local politician turned up with a TV cameraman to try to claim public credit for what had been done to assist.*

*Edith Wilkins Street Children Foundation / Railway Children - Calcutta*

This catalogue of woes seems grim. Despite such risks, it is remarkable how resilient some street children seem to be. Some of course do not survive. But many others cope with the exposure to disease and injury and seem hardened by it. Some children do take advantage of the attempts by NGOs to support them. NGO staff take such children to hospital and become accountable for them. Many programmes have a sick bay, perhaps a resident nurse, and many have a philanthropic doctor who will visit the project and dispense medicine in his own time and at his own cost. One NGO I knew (27) trained some of the street children in first aid and each week nominated one of them to be 'doctor' for the week on the local railway station, equipping the chosen boy or girl with a first aid box. That same NGO then persuaded a couple of doctors from the local private hospital to hold a surgery in the station concourse twice a week amid the swirling throng of people buying train tickets - the waiting room was a carpet on the stone floor - serving up to twenty or so street children from around the station every day they came.

# Chapter 7
## *Education*

UN Convention on the Rights of the Child, Article 28: 'State Parties recognize the right of the child to education, and with a view to achieving this right progressively and on the basis of equal opportunity, they shall in particular:

a) Make primary education compulsory and available free to all;

b) Encourage the development of different forms of secondary education, including general and vocational education, make them available and accessible to every child, and take appropriate measures such as the introduction of free education and offering financial assistance in case of need.

e) Take measures to encourage regular attendance at schools and the reduction of drop-out rates.'

Photograph by Dario Mitidieri

Many street children who live in slums and spend the majority of the day on the street do not, almost by definition, go to school. For many children, there is no school to go to, or it is of poor quality or there are no regular teachers. For others, the poverty of the family drives the children to seek a means of supplementing the family income, and they drift away from school or are forced to leave school to earn money. Thus, the short term need to survive obstructs the long term need to be sufficiently educated to get the qualifications necessary to escape from abject poverty, and the cycle continues.

Many of the children who enrol in primary schools do not complete the course, drop out or run away. Many, as previously mentioned, will be pressured by their families to support the family income out of economic necessity. Many cannot afford the minimal payments involved in schooling - uniforms, books and in some places, school fees. Other children run from school or attend irregularly because of the violence or bullying they encounter there. Many schools still employ corporal punishment not only as discipline for poor behaviour but also for perceived poor work. The study by the Indian Ministry of Women & Child Development (17), quoted in a previous chapter, identified the prevalent use of corporal punishment in many states, particularly for children aged between 5 and 12. Many children give beatings received at school as the reason for taking to the street.

The completion of primary education and advancement to secondary education is seen as vital for the long term prospects of children and in countries where this has been difficult, one finds that most children are eager for such an opportunity. As well as providing income generating prospects for all children, the education of girls also improves family wellbeing and health and provides the necessary encouragement to provide education for their children. Given these principles, most NGOs working with street children give enormous importance to providing the children they encounter with some sort of education, even if in the first instance it is only the ability to read and write basics in their own language.

Many NGOs therefore - especially the large international organisations, often working co-operatively with government education departments - provide non-formal educational facilities in the slums. Many smaller NGOs do similarly in specific local slum communities. Such facilities are usually primitive in that buildings are often of a temporary and flimsy nature and basically consist of one room, one teacher and a multitude of children aged anything between five and twelve years. It is difficult in such circumstances to keep track and monitor the achievements of individual children. Often such children are migrants and their families move on. Other children are irregular in attendance as they give priority to opportunities to earn money. Sometimes the slum and school is on land where the squatters are illegal and the landowner or municipal authority decide to move in with bulldozers and clear the settlement. The community scatters and such investment in the children's education becomes lost. In some street kid communities, including those on refuse dumps that are hard to reach in Cambodia, a local NGO (28) sends out a yellow minivan that provides literacy lessons, rights education, medical care and games and recreation.

Part of the objective of such non-formal education is to equip the children for 'mainstreaming' to national education system schools. Most NGOs will keep records of children mainstreamed and some will follow up and record the drop-out rate. The Indian government has developed a 'Bridge Course' intended for use in non-formal schools to enable children to make the transition to formal education more effective. However, the pressures of the family economy often lead to children dropping out. Others find the change from informal child-centred learning in the NGO schools to the often traditional large classes and rote learning, exam culture, still encountered in many systems, too great a leap to make and fall away. Children living in slums often find it difficult to keep up, especially when homework becomes a necessity. Their home conditions are just not conducive to study. Some NGOs provide evening classes in the non-formal school locations to give additional tuition or just provide a space and light where a child can do its homework. One NGO that ran non-formal schools beside the tracks at a number of stations on a Kolkata suburban railway (29) found that the drop out rate was as high as 76% in the first year of mainstreaming and decided to provide the evening additional schooling facilities to address the problem. The following year, the drop out rate was only 12%.

A project many years ago in a slum in Nairobi decided to incentivise the children. The Director, somewhat foolhardily, offered the children mainstreamed from his project a mountain bike if they achieved a place in the top ten of their class in the first year of state schooling. He was appalled to find that he owed fifteen bikes in the first year (the children were spread over several class ages) for which he had insufficient funds. The teachers apparently were equally put out, because these 'illiterate' street children outperformed the children they'd been teaching regularly for years! The street children were of course highly motivated not just by the thought of the bikes but also their first opportunity to go to a 'proper' school. They were also highly competent at problem solving - they'd had a lot of essential practice on the streets - although in the following years they found the academic learning and perseverance needed for formal exams more taxing.

For children who have left home and taken to the streets full time, the situation is even harder. Such children rarely have the necessary documents to enable them to enrol in schools even if they wanted to. Many children do not even know their age or where they were born and have no birth registration. NGOs working for such children will usually try to take some basic schooling to where the children accumulate. This will involve a teacher or social worker - or even an ex street child street educator - sitting down with the children hanging around out in the open, or in a borrowed house, under a tree or other common location.

Some enterprising and innovative school locations have emerged. In India, because so many street children are found round India's vast railway system, a number of NGOs run 'platform schools'. At a pre-arranged time a teacher paid by the NGO will arrive on a designated platform on the station and the children will squat cross-legged on the platform for anything up to four hours - with appropriate breaks whenever a train pulls in, for the children will scramble up and go to earn money by carrying bags or scavenging for food or empty waterbottles in the train! The materials used will be primitive - old newspapers and crayons, a few highly coloured posters - and activities will involve role play, story telling, drawing and painting as well as learning the alphabet and numbers. In such circumstances, the teacher or social worker will use the opportunity to try to establish each child's reason for being on the street and try to help them see options for future development away from their present circumstances. In Dhaka in Bangladesh, one enterprising NGO (30) has negotiated a school on a ferry with the local ferry company - one ferry is usually in dock under routine repair and the company allows a room on this ferry to become the non-formal school for children in the dock area until the ship is ready for sailing and is replaced by another due maintenance.

More NGOs are now putting efforts into the stemming of children taking to the street by engaging with children in rural schools and teaching them about their rights and the risks children face on the streets including the lures of traffickers. For example, in the Indian State of Bihar, one of the poorest and where literacy levels are well below 50%, a number of NGOs provide after school recreation and child rights awareness in conjunction with the village community leaders and the women.

Other NGOs put such a priority on formal education that they either provide residential homes from which the children are taken to school regularly or even provide their own formal schools working to an approved curriculum. Future Hope in Kolkata has four such schools for different age groups, boys and girls, where academic achievement is prized. A school in a children's village in Vijayawada in south east India (31) regularly puts its older boys through Standard 12 exams and many go on to university. A project run by a nun in the central Indian state of Madhya Pradesh (32) targets young girls living with their families around the railway station or on the street, girls at high risk of being trafficked, and then houses them in a residential centre by the station and ensures their daily attendance at a good private school, while they maintain contact with their families being remaining close by. Other NGOs without residential facilities with which to support children attending mainstream schools offer placement in boarding schools to children who have no adequate or suitable family home.

Of course, many street children have never had the opportunity for formal learning or have dropped out of education in the first or second years of schooling. It is not effective or reasonable to expect a 13 or 14 year old boy to sit down with six or seven year old children to learn to read and write, so most NGOs provide the opportunity to learn a skill or trade - vocational training. This will usually involve enough academic training in writing and arithmetic to be able to conduct a small business - to assess stock levels or account for income (a lot of street children seem to have acquired this knack without any academic learning!). Many NGOs now help children to run a children's bank, partly to enable them to save in a place they trust and partly as 'on the job' learning of simple mathematics.

The traditional skills taught to children in such situations are sewing and tailoring, vehicle maintenance - especially cycles and motor cycles - carpentry, toy making, candle making, craftwork and screen printing. NGOs need to be aware of employment trends so that they teach children skills that will be in demand in the future and in India training in computer programming and the ability to create websites or undertake the making of menus, business cards, wedding invitations and the like are now well established. Other skill training involves driver training - one Mumbai based NGO (33) trained twenty ex street girls to be the first women taxi drivers in the city where they are now much in demand. The same NGO got the local police to train 50 young street women to be security guards in factories where mainly women were employed. In Nairobi a local NGO (34) has formed associations of children on the street, trained them in leadership, team work and some vocational skills, then helped them find legitimate work appropriate to the area where they lived. For example, they discovered that one group of youths hung around a bus station and occasional got tips for cleaning buses. The NGO got the bus company to train the children and then employ them as bus cleaners on a proper footing.

One NGO in Darjeeling (35) was doing the traditional vocational training for girls who had been trafficked over the borders from Nepal, Bhutan, Sikkim and Bangladesh - sewing in particular - but they found this repetitive and not always adequate for the girls' needs. They brought in an educational psychologist to find alternative ways of teaching the children, using concentration exercises and games, behavioural and anger management. Music became a huge part of the programme and unexpectedly, the project team found that children who learned string instruments did very well. They introduced the children to classical music, found this very healing, and now teach the children to play the violin, guitar and various percussion instruments. Learning music together is great for helping them to play as a team and creates a bond between the children. This same project rescues many girls from the sex trade and as the children are used to being 'made up', they are turning their experiences around by teaching them beautician's skills and they are now receiving commissions for guests and the principals at weddings. Nurse training is another very fulfilling skill for the girls - helping others to recover from sickness is a healing process for themselves.

What do the children say about their education?

*'Me mam and dad didn't care if we went to school or not so sometimes we went and sometimes we didn't. We moved around a lot when we were little so education was disrupted and we got into the habit of missing school. I'd have liked to have gone to school properly, get some qualifications and that.'*

**15 year old boy, Northern Ireland - Railway Children**

*Boupha is 16 years old. Her family lives in an extremely poor area of Sihanoukville, Cambodia. She no longer lives at home as her mother gambles and her father is violent. In the past, Boupha would miss school to look after her younger sisters and was often forced to sell vegetables to help support the family. 'I worried that because I had missed so much school I would never get a good job and my family would always struggle. I saw my future full of poverty, fear and sadness. I felt afraid to stick up for myself and fight for my right to education. My dream has always been the same, to own my own land and house so I can look after my parents and sisters. I want to have a job so that I can earn a safe income and feel proud to have skills that support me and my family.'*

*Boupha first heard about M'Lop Tapang, an NGO with an extensive programme to over 600 street children, through its outreach work in the community. The outreach team encouraged Boupha to visit the drop-in centre, where she was able to share her problems with a trained counsellor.*

*'It gave me hope, confidence and stopped my feeling of fear and isolation. These people seemed to understand me and never passed judgment. It seemed they were very experienced at listening to my problems and offering me and others many choices to improve our lives. I knew that my life would change now that I had a chance and a channel into learning.'*

*Having returned to school to finish her studies, Boupha recently completed an embroidery course at M'Lop Tapang's new vocational training centre. She is now hoping to start work at its small retail outlet by the beach, which provides a safe and steady form of income generation, particularly for those who are forced to work and beg on the streets. Without this help, Boupha thinks she would have ended up working in one of Sihanoukville's karaoke bars, which can often lead to work in the sex industry. She is currently staying at the night shelter for girls but,*

with help from M'Lop Tapang, she hopes to return home soon. 'When I have saved up enough money I would like to buy my own sewing machine and set up my own independent business - I would love to train former street youths like myself so they get a chance like I have now.'
**Boupha, Cambodia, International Childcare Trust**

Javier had been living between the street and his home for quite some time as it was preferable to being neglected and ignored at home by his mother. When his mother moved to live with her boyfriend leaving him and an older brother alone, he moved out altogether. He was soon in trouble with the police for stealing and was eventually sent to the State Detention Centre. There he met Juconi´s educator and started to work towards being allowed to move to Juconi House, a half-way residential programme to prepare children and their families for reintegration.

In Juconi House Javier was aggressive, quick to take offence and constantly challenging educators. In individual therapeutic sessions, Javier´s educator introduced play therapy using sand trays to see if it could help him to explore his experiences and feelings about them. Gradually, Javier revealed a childhood of loss, fear and abandonment.

Javier had not got beyond 2nd grade of primary school and at 11 was illiterate. He found learning in a small group very difficult to manage, but responded well to one on one sessions. Learning to read and write seemed to give him confidence and he was keen to go to school. Educators used this to help motivate him to manage his behaviour and he soon started in a compensatory primary school programme where he was able to complete 2 school grades each year. He made friends at school and in Juconi House his violent outbursts and tantrums became fewer and he became more cooperative to the point where he was happy to help younger children with their homework.

Javier stayed in Juconi House for just over 3 years during which time the team of family educators worked intensively with his mother and her partner. He has been back with his mother for a year and is now in 2nd grade of secondary school. His favourite subject is science and his ambition is to be a teacher or computer programmer.
**Javier, Puebla - Juconi**

The children are fanatical about music usually the local Pop & Hindi music, and when some of the local community approached us re teaching the children classical music we decided to go with it and see how they did. The children were totally **not** interested initially, so we got these guys to hold a concert for them, (after we had spent some

64

time introducing them to classical music, both Indian & Western). When they saw the instruments making the music they had heard they were stunned! Some of our children who were hard core kids were literally glued to their seats. Afterwards there were two of them that had to go and feel the violins and just hold them, both these kids were from very disturbed backgrounds. There isn't really an explanation, besides the fact that kids have to sit still and really concentrate on string instruments to learn to play them, but with violins in particular children who play them do particularly well academically.

When we were officially opening the houses, the children were only playing the instruments for a few weeks and had mastered playing the Indian /Irish national anthems which they played in front of the Irish ambassador to India. And then to the Director General of Police, West Bengal, with hundreds of people there. Some people say teaching the children Mozart is off the wall, we find teaching them classical music brings out so much good in them, their studies improve enormously and they are rehabilitated & come to terms with what has happened to them so much more quickly.

For example, when you teach the children gardening and bring plants and animals into their lives they are so placid and gentle with them (is it I wonder that they are creating something so beautiful and feel inside 'yes I can do something beautiful' or the instruments, plants and animals give them no beatings or abuse, when they give love, they receive something beautiful in return). Whatever it is, it works wonders on the children who have spent their whole lives being abused, tortured, belittled, and suddenly they turn a corner for us. There's still a lot of work and counselling to do with them, but again they become more receptive, open and calmer to deal with and seem to heal quicker, when they eventually realise there's a whole world there for them to explore and enjoy. A whole new world where they can get their childhood back go to school and stop having to look over their shoulder to make sure no one is going to abuse them anymore, it's a wonderful sight to see.

**Edith Wilkins – Darjeeling**


Ramesh is now fourteen years old. Originally from a district in the east of Nepal, he migrated with his family to Pokhara many years ago due to poverty and lived in a slum area of the city. He has three siblings and lived at home with his mother and step-father. The step-father is an alcoholic and works as a manual labourer with a daily wage while his mother sells vegetables. When they arrived in Pokhara,

65

*Ramesh enrolled into a local government school to continue his education. However due to their poor economic condition and the behaviour of his step-father Ramesh could not get money to buy the educational materials he needed for school (uniform, books etc.). At first during the holidays and then before and after school Ramesh began to rag-pick to buy these materials and earn some pocket money. The behaviour of his step-father began to deteriorate even further and he began to beat Ramesh. This, combined with Ramesh's increasing relations with street children from his work, resulted in Ramesh running away and he started to live full-time on the street. He was 11 years old. On the street Ramesh began to smoke and regularly use glue. He started to sleep in a scrap centre and he became a frequent victim of sexual abuse from older street children. This increased to such an extent that Ramesh began to "voluntarily" engage in sexual abuse to earn money at times. At the same time, and in response to his situation, Ramesh's behaviour deteriorated further and he spent more time in isolation from all except his immediate peer group.*

*Identified by staff at Kidasha's local partner, Jyoti Street Project, they began to meet him regularly in outreach and work to motivate him to visit the contact centre. Over a period of time he began to visit the centre (initially just for the afternoon snack) but slowly he became involved in different activities in the centre, in particular the Children's Development Khajana (bank). His confidence and motivation grew and he progressed to become a bank manager and a member of the management committee. Ramesh was finally supported to return to his family after it was identified that the situation had changed in particular due to the increasing age of his older brother who took more control in the family and also came to look for Ramesh. Back in school Ramesh was again studying in Class 5, but again he left home after two months. The adjustment back into family life proved a challenge for him. Back on the street again project staff again invested significant time in counselling Ramesh. Over a period of three months they were able to motivate him again to return to his family but also to develop his skills to be able to deal with the change and to improve his attitude towards social norms.*

*Ramesh is now back in school and at home and has been there for five months. His progress is extremely positive and he is in regular contact with his social worker. It is hoped he will not have to run away from*

*home again. But if he does fall he knows where to find help getting up again.*
**Ramesh, Nepal,- Kidasha**


'*When I went to my mother, my father would take me away and if I went to my father, my mother came to take me, so I had no direction. I was spinning like that and I couldn't study because of that.*
**Street Boy, East Africa – Railway Children**

'*My life is hard. To eat I must work and my mother sneers at me – every time I remind her about going to school, she tells me that I should go but she doesn't do anything and when I ask her, she becomes furious ... She blasts me.*'
**David, East Africa – Railway Children**

'*I was sent home from school for fees, I feared going to disturb my mother ... I just left because of the school fees. Also the uniform contributed towards my leaving home. I had to cut my trousers to get a pair of shorts.*'
**Ouga, East Africa – Railway Children**

'*I was also studying, but my elder brother and I were expelled because we didn't have a pair of trousers for school.*'
**Street Boy, East Africa – Railway Children**

'*You know, at that time people paid for school. You know that if you haven't finished paying your school fees, you can't finish your exams, they will stop you from many things at school and you'll be sent away.*'
**James, Kenya – Railway Children**

'*I like to go to school so that later I can get my life. I can become a guard or ... I could become like Obama.*'
**Young Street Boy, Kenya – Railway Children**

**Whilst much activity takes place worldwide to improve access for street children to the different types of education, too little is documented about the success rate of these programmes. As well as knowing how many children have been mainstreamed to formal education, NGOs need to**

67

monitor how long they remain in education and the qualifications they attain. They need to know not just how many children go through vocational training courses, but monitor how many then get jobs and whether they are able to hold them down. Many different types of education are appropriate for street children in different circumstances but we need to learn the most effective experiences of these different educational options.

# Chapter 8
## *Play*

UN Convention on the Rights of the Child, Article 31 (1):
'State Parties recognize the right of the child to rest and leisure, to engage in play and recreational activities appropriate to the age of the child and to participate freely in cultural life and the arts.'

**Photograph by Marcus Lyon**

There are few planned opportunities for recreation and play for children living in the slums. There are rarely any open spaces where children can congregate and play football or cricket or other ball games. The homes and shacks are so small and crowded that there is no room for a child to play. At best, if the slum has an electricity supply, even an illegal one, there may be a television set round which children will gather. In any case, most children in the slums, if they are not attending a school, spend their time in the alleyways searching for the opportunity to earn a few coins. Of course, children, even with no proper resources, can always invent their own amusement with the most primitive materials. Puddles of stagnant water after monsoon rains, discarded bits of metal, old tyres can all be brought into play. And of course, children react with each other, chanting ritual verses, singing, dancing, competing, fighting, swimming in dirty pools of water as the street children in the film 'Slumdog Millionaire' did with such verve.

In some slums, small non formal schools run by NGOs will provide an opportunity for recreation. Lessons will include drawing, singing, dancing. Visitors will usually be entertained with 'party pieces' the children have learned, popular songs, a poem, the re-creation of a folk myth in mime. And the children enjoy each other's company and interaction with a sympathetic adult.

Children living on the streets of the cities of the world have more freedom, fewer restrictions and more scope, although the recreations they invent hold many risks as well as pleasures. These children can choose where they congregate - until some authoritarian figure moves them on - and they find the open spaces, parks and wide streets, derelict sites, and river banks, or sandy beaches. They gather in the markets, on railway platforms, under trees and sit in huddles gambling away their few accumulated coins. They spend the money they've somehow acquired, after filling their bellies, on a trip to the local cinema if they can afford it, to see a Western or a Bollywood epic and mimic the shoot outs and learn the popular songs of the moment. They hang around places of public access where there is a television that can be spied on, even if it's only showing non-stop adverts. They find a rough patch of fairly level ground and purloin a makeshift football, or gather round a chalked wicket on a crumbling wall and thrash a battered tennis ball with an improvised bat, a remnant of wood levered off some ramshackle shed. They plunge into lakes and rivers, or the sea, fully clothed or naked. They just hang out together. They laugh, they cry, they comfort one another, they experiment with each other's bodies. They inhale intoxicants, they smoke cigarettes, they have sex.

If an NGO wishes to engage with such children, as a first step in offering the child a different option, it has to provide some alternative draw. As well as the basic necessities of food, medicines for ailments, a wash and clean clothes, entertainment to attract the children is vital. Most shelters for such children will have a television, and often a computer on which games can be played by the children. Some will have educational toys or board games. In India a favourite is the Carrom Board, originally a gambling game - a cross between snooker, draughts and tiddly-winks! And the children will be encouraged to sing and act and dance, often as an informal means of basic education.

In children's residential homes, there is scope for more active entertainment. Many NGOs develop the children's artistic abilities; there is a stage for children to perform. For street children who have experienced rejection and whose self-respect is low, such opportunities rebuild confidence and the feeling of being of value. I have seen spectacular dancing and acrobatics in projects I have visited and seen comedies acted out, which I failed to understand because of the language barrier, while audiences of children rocked with laughter. I have seen exhibitions of drawings and paintings, some with great artistic flair, decorating the walls of the home. The children have the space and opportunity to join in team games, races, organised sports supervised by someone who curbs their excesses and ensures some order to give shape to the game.

In south India, a couple of State cricketers held a series of nets with 150 street children from a number of NGOs in the city. Famous sportsmen have taken a direct interest in street children and have participated with them - Steve Waugh, the former Australian cricket captain, took an ongoing involvement during an test tour in India and Saurav Ganguly, the former Indian test captain is closely associated with an NGO in Kolkata. There are well known footballers too, and Pele, who came from a humble background himself, has been a role model for Brazilian street youth. The British Trust, Comic Relief, developed Sport Relief with the BBC and sent a team of celebrities to play cricket with tsunami affected children on the beaches of south east India, and then later played a match against Bollywood celebrities in the huge Bombay Stadium before thousands of children. But more importantly Andrew Flintoff, who was in India with the England Test team at the time, played alley cricket with children from an NGO in the back streets of Mumbai, and I'm told, was even cleaned bowled by one youngster, though to my disappointment the BBC failed to show that clip!

One of the NGO members of Consortium for Street Children (The Amos Trust) organised a Street Children World Cup in Durban in 2010 to coincide with the Football World Cup in South Africa, and inviting street children from NGOs in eight countries to send a national team of street children to compete. Teams from South Africa, Tanzania, the Philippines, India, Ukraine, Nicaragua, Brazil and the UK competed and India beat Tanzania in the Final. As well as providing opportunities and entertainment in sport for these selected few, there was a great opportunity to create worldwide awareness of street children and campaign for their rights – indeed, the clearing up of street children from the streets of Durban by the police was filmed by visiting media and led to actions by the city authorities to stop the practice then and during the Football World Cup a few months later. The same organisation is now planning a bigger event around the 2014 World Cup in Brazil, inviting the street children of some twenty countries to compete and make their voices heard in a conference and rights campaign at the same time.

Comic Relief, with their joint fundraising initiative, Sport Relief, researched the impact that sport can make in the rehabilitation of street children (36). Sport can be a valuable tool in the development of street children programmes where it is part of a broader agenda of change. It can help to engage and retain hard-to-reach groups of children. It can create a safe, structured space where these groups are able to build the relationships of trust they need to address their problems. And it can enable them to experience some of the specific physical and psychological health benefits associated with physical exercise. However, sport alone cannot address the complex problems faced by many disadvantaged children around the world.

Sport, where it involves regular physical activity, contributes to a range of physical and some psychological health benefits. To maximise these benefits for poor and disadvantaged children, programmes need to target specific groups, match participants' skills to the activity and use local facilities to encourage long-term participation and strengthen the social side of sport. Sport is also a very strong 'hook' to attract children in to hear health messages, but studies so far provide no robust evidence of actual change in behaviour. There is anecdotal evidence that the physical nature of sports can provide a useful entry point to discussions about sensitive health issues where the programmes are local and there are strong and positive relationships built between coaches and peers. However, as yet there are no proven direct causal links between sport and reduction in crime, substance abuse or other anti-social behaviour. Sport can provide, however, many of the 'protective factors' that reduce the risk of youth engaging in those behaviours. These include close contact with caring adults, opportunities for positive group interaction, explicit training in team work and conflict resolution, provision of a 'safe space' to spend time, a voluntary and outreach approach that is local, based on participants' identified needs and provides linkages to educational and employment opportunities.

It is revealing and perhaps significant that there are very few references to sport, games or entertainment in any of the quotations from street children involved in the research reports used in this book. Did the children not have time to play games? Was it not important for them? Or didn't the researchers ask questions about how they entertained themselves? When I have visited projects I have immediately been drawn in to participate in the children's entertainment. I have played (and lost) many times at 'Carrom Board'. I still have battered finger nails from playing cricket on my last trip to India – you see children playing improvised cricket on every vacant patch of land in the cities, sometimes two or even three matches overlapping. And I still shudder at my ineptitude at dancing at which girls in more than one programme laugh hilariously. So, without, their direct

73

voices, I offer a few examples that have been offered by Consortium members or which I've come across myself:

*It is hard to imagine receiving daily beatings, and that your own mother would respond to almost any question with nothing but a slap and look of disgust. This is what 13 year old Paul endured before running away from home to the streets of Kampala. He survived on the streets the best way he could, begging and sleeping rough, but often had to turn to drugs, petty crime and violence just to survive. The days rolled into months, and months into years, until it was two and a half years later and he had no education to speak of and a bleak future ahead of him.*

*When Retrak first encountered Paul in 2007 he was withdrawn and quiet, he distrusted adults and shied away from any type of help offered. Staff had no idea of the trauma he had experienced at home, or whilst living on the streets. Luckily, he had been introduced to Retrak by his fellow street friends who had told him about the weekly football matches. Paul loved sport and quickly took the opportunity to escape street life and just play with his friends. Over time Paul got to know the staff team who gained his trust and encouraged him to engage in a long term programme which would give him a real alternative to life on the streets. He started to attend the drop in centre on a regular basis, showed great promise in his catch up lessons and was eager to rebuild his life. However, despite having counselling Paul had no desire to return home or be resettled into his local community, instead he said that he wanted to stand on his own two feet and that Retrak had given him the confidence to pursue his studies and undertake vocational training.*

*Paul lived at the organisation's hostel in Kampala and studied Electrical Installation. He impressed his teachers and industry mentors throughout his training and upon graduating obtained employment for a company in Entebbe. Vocational training equipped Paul with the skills and knowledge necessary to live happily and independently in society.*
### Paul, Uganda - Retrak

*In a few exceptional cases, the sporting skills of the children are more professionally developed. There is a street children home in Kolkata where the Director is a sports enthusiast with a background himself of playing rugby at a high level. He has inspired some of his boys to form*

74

a youth rugby team that has swept away all competition in 'sevens' events and the like. After beating a police team in one final, the police sports trainer invited the NGO to send a couple of their older boys to coach their police youth team. The Director impressed upon the boys that they must conduct themselves appropriately in such company and was a little alarmed to see the two boys convulsed in laughter on their return. Somewhat apprehensively he enquired what had happened, and in between the giggles, they said, 'They called us 'Sir'! The police actually called us 'Sir'!' That same home has encouraged other children to play tennis competently and several years ago two of the younger child potential stars were invited to sit in the royal box at Wimbledon and one of them tossed the coin for the Women's Final. A more lasting outcome is that - at the latest update - ten former street children had graduated to be qualified as professional sports coaches in football, rugby and cricket.

**Future Hope, Calcutta**

Another NGO in Delhi uses sport deliberately as part of their efforts to discourage drug taking, or to wean the children from the habit. They have formed football teams to take part in a local league and the children know that if they are under the influence of inhalants they will not be selected to play in the team.

**Butterflies, Delhi**

There is a boys' village in Vijayawada in India where the former street children have access to a beach on the River Krishna and the Director has a boat – both of which provide recreational facilities for all the children, led by some of the older boys. And they have contact with skilled drama and dance professionals who encourage and train the youngsters to put on spectacular concerts for the other children and visitors, restoring self-confidence and respect. Watching them and participating in their activities, it is hard to visualise their life at the local railway junction from which many had so recently escaped.

**SKCV/Railway Children – Vijayawada, India**

There is limited evidence to show that sport *per se* can lead to many of the benefits associated with it. It demonstrates, however, that sport has qualities that can make it a valuable tool in development. Its popularity makes it an effective way to 'hook' children into broader programmes, but more importantly, it can engage them longer-term by creating a safe place in which relationships of trust can develop in a non-threatening environment. Sports brings opportunities to mix across generations, build relationships through both verbal and non-verbal communication, bring structure and enable children to experience some of the physical and psychological health benefits associated with physical exercise.   And the street children have the right to play and be a child, just like any other child. The street forces them to grow up too quickly. They need space to relax and be a child again.

# Chapter 9
## *Hope*

UN Convention on the Rights of the Child, Article 29: 'State Parties agree that the education of the child shall be directed to:

a) The development of the child's personality, talents and mental and physical abilities to their fullest potential;

b) The development of respect for human rights and fundamental freedoms for the principles enshrined in the Charter of the United Nations;

d) The preparation of the child for responsible life in a free society, in the spirit of understanding, peace, tolerance, equality of sexes, and friendship among all peoples, ethnic, national and religious groups and persons of indigenous origins.'

**Photograph by Marcus Lyon**

The UN Convention on the Rights of the Child celebrated its 21st Anniversary on the 20th November 2010. It is the UN treaty that has been signed and ratified by more countries than any other such instrument. Only two of the 193 nations making up the UN have yet to ratify - Somalia and the United States. There have been a number of events, including conferences, marking the anniversary, and at most similar evaluations have been made - that progress on children's rights in most countries has been made in the legislative framework, but the implementation is patchy and in some countries woefully weak.

Efforts are being made by some governments to draw up national plans for vulnerable children, including street children. India has put in place an Integrated Child Protection System, which is in the process of implementation and has set up a National Commission for the Protection of Children's Rights, although the task ahead of that country to ensure all children are afforded their rights is immense. Tanzania is developing a national plan for street children, following surveys and a conference in conjunction with the British Consortium for Street Children and some of its members. The UK has issued in consultation with a number of British NGOs, including a member of the Consortium for Street Children, Railway Children, guidance to local authorities on planning services to support runaway children and address their vulnerability.

There are many international and national NGOs devoted to supporting and improving the lot of vulnerable children, including street children. Some of the larger international NGOs focus on campaigning and channelling their resources through national governments, particularly in the areas of health and education. Such programmes in city slums and rural areas, whilst not directly addressing the issue of street children, are putting in place improvements in protection and child development which ought to reduce the likelihood of children running from their homes and communities from ignorance, fear and abuse. Other smaller NGOs are more clearly focussed to the specific problems faced by street children. Most of these are nationally based and run by local people. In the mega cities of Latin America and South Asia there are many such NGOs - some belonging to networks which try to co-ordinate their services and share information and good practice. Western European and North American NGOs link up with such national NGOs in partnership providing much needed funds, as well as know-how and exposure to the international context. In the UK, over sixty NGOs, most focussed specifically on street children, belong to Consortium for Street Children and these NGOs have partners working in over 120 countries of the world.

The NGOs working for street children provide between them, although unfortunately not comprehensively, a whole range of services and development opportunities for the children. Some offer welfare services - immediate emergency help by providing food, medical care and some form of protection which might have a base in a drop-in centre or night shelter. Some provide residential care for the most vulnerable children, which includes their education as well as welfare needs. Many provide welfare services and address the longer term development needs of the child, be it academic or vocational education, the acquisition of life skills and a positive relationship with society. All have to start with recognising the needs of individual children which are unique to each child, although in most cases a child's experience of being unwanted or rejected has to be faced first of all, and the self-worth, confidence and trust of the child has to be restored. Street children live for the day, and few give thought for the morrow - they are too busy trying to survive each day, finding food, shelter and friends, and too often seeking refuge from their plight by indulging in harmful or wasteful pursuits. One objective, therefore, for NGOs working particularly with runaway and abused children is to give them hope - a perspective beyond the immediate, so that they will value the opportunities that may be offered to them and cease to give immediate satisfaction their priority.

Many NGOs do not find such support sufficient, even when they are providing development opportunities as well as meeting welfare needs. Increasingly they recognise that they need to lobby governments to provide the necessary infrastructure to meet the needs of the most vulnerable children, provide the community support that makes the abuse and exploitation of such children less likely and provide a safety net for those children who still need special treatment. They can demonstrate to governments the impact of innovative programmes and projects that make a positive difference and encourage the replication and application of such learning by larger NGOs and government ministries on a wider scale.

NGOs specialise as well in the specific groups of children they support, sometimes by geography and also by the nature of the child - some work by reaching out to the newest children just taking to the street and seeking to offer help and possible family restoration before a child is abused, exploited or corrupted on the street. Some work in the slum and rural communities seeking to provide the services and conditions to prevent children taking to the street. Some work with older street youth, with children who have been traumatised by their experiences and sought refuge in drugs and alcohol. Some work with the girls, who - while less obvious on the street - are the most vulnerable of all. Some recognise that children have come to the cities primarily to earn money and concentrate on training these children in marketable skills so that they may be self-sufficient. Some work on income generation with a whole community. Some work with child labourers, with the scavengers operating on the rubbish tips of the world, some work with street children who are disabled or infected with HIV/AIDS or the other diseases that street children are prone to.

Many of the earlier chapters of this book focus on the problems and challenges street children face in their daily lives. Many of us would not give much chance for a successful outcome if we were in the situation these children are. We look at our own children and shudder to think what would happen if they were left to fend for themselves at eight or ten years of age. Yet it has been said several times that many street children have extraordinary resilience that they've built up in their determination to survive. They are children who have not been prepared to accept life's problems passively, but have rebelled against the circumstances of their lives. Given the opportunity and some real affection and respect from a sympathetic and resourceful adult, whether as an individual or part of a caring NGO, many children not only turn into useful and self-sufficient members of society able to hold down a job, and successfully raise a family of their own, but many have moved on to distinguish themselves in different walks of life. The rest of this chapter will highlight some of the stories of such children which give hope to other children and to those who would inspire them.

*Sovann was hanging around in the slums of Sihanoukville. He had dropped out of school four years earlier and didn't know what he wanted to do with his life. He met a social worker from the local NGO M'Lop Tapang and, after a few weeks, developed a close rapport with him. Eventually Sovann decided to visit the vocational training centre and soon enrolled on the welding course. He was a quick learner and showed real commitment to his work. When the M'Lop Tapang arts centre needed an assistant technician, he was offered the position. After a three month trial he has now been made a full time junior technician. 'I am so proud to be part of the arts programme and to be learning from staff who are so skilled. I am very happy as I have a bright future now... I hope to work in this forever.'*

**Sovann, Cambodia - International Childcare Trust**

*Lucy's mother has long-term mental health issues and misuses alcohol as does her father who physically and emotionally abused the whole family.*

*'Basically my first memory is of me, my brother and me wee sister jumping on the bed and my dad came in and battered us all. He used to batter us kids and he used to batter my mum.'*

*Lucy's father broke her brother's nose and Lucy and told a teacher who contacted social services. Lucy and her family had previously been involved with social services but had ceased to be involved with them:*

*'We were supposed to be doing really well but we weren't really; the social work thought we were so we got taken off supervision and then .... we got back with social services supervision and then not long after that, my dad battered my mum. It was really bad.'*

*After this incident, Lucy and her siblings were placed in foster care for a year and a half. Lucy's father left her mother and Lucy and her sister returned to live with their mother. However, this did not last long:*

*'Me and me sister actually asked to be put somewhere else because we couldn't handle it: my mum started turning against us ... She was being violent; she nearly broke my arm ... she was drinking us and was just depressed about my dad being away and that.'*

*Whilst living in the second foster care placement, Lucy and her sister wanted to return to live with their mother but social services would not allow them to do so:*

*'We got supervised visits and we weren't allowed to be there with my mum on our own. We were allowed to go and see my father; they were alright about that.'*

*Lucy's younger sister, who gets on well with their father, then wanted to live with their father:*

81

'She talked me round to moving in with me dad. They [social services] thought it was a great idea and my dad was doing really well: he got the room decorated for us and stuff like that.'

At first things went well but, after a few weeks, Lucy's father began to be aggressive and Lucy was forced to care for her sister and father. When Lucy was fourteen, as a response to their father's aggression, Lucy and her sister ran away for six weeks and stayed with a number of Lucy's friends. Lucy missed school during this time but there was no enquiry about this absence when she returned to school. This incident of being away ended when Lucy and her sister went to see their former fostercarers who contacted social services. Lucy and her sister insisted that they did not want to return to live with their father but social services said there was nowhere for them to go where they could remain together. However, social services set respite care in place and Lucy's father received support to manage his anger. Lucy recognises that that there have been consequences of her experiences at home:

'Concentration was affected; sleep was affected; stuff like that. I sometimes had nightmares. I still have them now... I have nightmares about my dad hitting my mum and waking up in cold sweat; stuff like that.'

Lucy now lives in her own flat, volunteers at a runaways project and plans to go to university to train to be a social worker. She has very little contact with her father and acts as a carer for her mother. Like so many ex-street children, she is a very resilient girl and now offers much to others.

### Lucy, England – Railway Children

A large crowd of NGO delegates to the 1999 Durban Commonwealth Conference stood spellbound in the exhibition hall when a young voice was heard, singing into the microphone in the clearest possible voice about his sorrow being an AIDS orphan living on the streets of Durban. His father had died, his mother remarried a man who beat him and then his mother died. I was present as a member of the British Parliamentary delegation and was so moved, I went straight to the stand of the BBC World Service and begged them to listen to this 8 year old child with the voice of an angel. They did and were captivated.

Brandon was recorded by them and sang at the World Service New Year concert a song his aunt wrote for him. During the interval I spoke to Chief Bhutelezi of the Zulu tribe and told him of the young Zulu street child, whose life expectancy was so low at that time. The Chief was moved and arranged for Brandon to join his own children for singing lessons with Joseph Shabala, lead singer of the Black Mambazo band. As a result Chief Bhutelezi made an announcement that he was starting a fund in support of musically gifted Zulu children. Joseph Shabala agreed to audition Brandon and subsequently I heard that he had great singing and dancing talent. He had taken Brandon into his own family and taught him with the Chief's children.

During the Millennium fireworks display, the TV suddenly burst out with the Black Mambazo band performing in the Dome – this was followed by a phone call to me from Brandon, shouting excitedly 'I'm here, I'm here, I'm in London !'

**Trudy Davies, Co-Founder of the Consortium for Street Children & Parliamentary Lobbyist.**

From infancy Adam was neglected by his parents, spending long periods shut in his room and subject to extreme physical abuse by his father. His parents were involved with drugs and his mother had a mental health disorder. When he was four he was placed in foster care, but when he was nine he and his sister were returned from the caring foster parents to live with his father again who started to sexually abuse the girl and physically abuse Adam. He rebelled and became involved with the police. He was returned to his foster parents but by this time his behaviour had changed drastically and they couldn't cope. He then went through four different foster arrangements and finally, aged thirteen, ran to the woods to find his own space. By fifteen he was involved in drinking and committing crimes. When he was sixteen he was placed under the care of a social worker who cared about him. Adam says: 'He spoke to you more as a person than a client. He was more easygoing; you could chat to him about anything. He was good. He helped me a lot. He got me off the streets and into a hostel... He helped me to go to college as well.'

While living in the hostel for the homeless, Adam is training to be a sports coach working with children and young people and does voluntary work in an old people's home and with disabled children. Adam would like to train as a social worker with children and young people and put his experiences to good use.

**Adam, England - Railway Children**

Mexican based NGO, Juconi, contacted the five Ramirez children, (Laura, Rosaura, Felipe, Juán and Eduardo) working long hours selling chewing gum at a traffic intersection. None of the children were in school though the three eldest had been to school intermittently. Juan and Eduardo did not have birth certificates. Neither parent worked and they lived in a dingy, two room house. Don Luis drank excessively and they fought constantly and Doña Margarita had required medical attention on occasions as a result. Doña Margarita explained her violence towards her children as her only means of keeping them in order so they would not anger their father/step-father. She described the children as being out of control and Felipe had threatened to hit her.

Juconi worked with the Ramirez family for 4.5 years, 2.5 of them intensively, visiting the family in their home every week to provide individual and family educational-therapeutic attention as well as helping them integrate into their local community through accompanying them in building relations with school teachers, health services and employers.

Eight years later, Juconi is in touch with the Ramirez family through the Tracking Programme which follows-up on children and families over ten years to see what impact Juconi's services have had. Laura is a single mum and her daughter goes to a local pre-school while she attends a government training course to become a hair dresser. Rosaura and Felipe both finished secondary school and have steady jobs. They bought a piece of land between them and have built Rosaura a 3-room house and are saving to build Felipe's. Juán is studying at technical college to become an electrician and Eduardo is in secondary school. They describe the family environment as relaxed and say that their parents get along well together. Living conditions are still cramped and money is very tight, but Don Luis no longer drinks and he and Margarita both work. They took their first family holiday together last year when they went to Veracruz to visit Don Luis' parents.

**The Ramirez Family, Puebla - Juconi**

Toybox has been pioneering a child Ambassador's scheme that enables street living, street working and high risk children to make their voice heard in the areas where they live, and internationally. Each of the indigenous projects that the NGO supports participates in the Ambassador scheme. The children who attend the project hold a democratic election once every two years at which they choose two of their peers as Ambassadors or representatives. These Ambassadors then participate in a range of activities which raise awareness about street living, working and high-risk children in the city where they live. After two years, another election is held so that other children have the opportunity to be Ambassadors.

Every month the Ambassadors in the city network come together to have a meeting and to decide on their aims and activities for the next month. The Ambassadors plan and carry out wide range of activities

84

including plays, debates, conferences, and the expressive arts. They also appear frequently on local radio, television and in the print media speaking about children in their country; including those living on the streets and the issues facing them.

The Child Ambassadors are uniquely placed to speak out about issues facing street children, because most of them have lived or worked on the streets before. They have a real passion for justice and a determination to change the situation of other children. Many of them come from very difficult and deprived backgrounds. The Ambassador scheme develops their confidence and leadership skills. Most importantly, the scheme allows former street children to have a voice and a positive, visible presence in the cities where there are many children still living on the streets.

### Child Ambassador's Scheme, Cochabamba, Bolivia - Toybox

Street children and children living in difficult circumstances, child labourers, all live and hang out in groups basically to survive and support each other. It's not the strongest or physically biggest kids that are the leaders of the group, it's the smartest that are the group leaders. They survive by fighting, protecting their own territory, and on the stations and streets, the children have blades under their tongues to be ready to fight and just survive. Darjeeling is the home to the Sherpa community (Tenzing Norgay who climbed Mount Everest with Edmund Hillary being born here). The huge Himalayan Mountaineering Institute is world famous, and the instructors got very involved with the children and the programmes as so many of them are natural climbers. The whole philosophy behind the children climbing was that they had to work in teams. If you are climbing a rock face, there is another person holding the rope and ensuring your safety, children who don't have great relationships or found it difficult to trust people, developed them in rock climbing. Their negative attitude changed to a positive team attitude when they discovered what they could do together, working as a team, instead of constantly being at each other's throats. The jealousies even disappeared when some children got picked to represent us in the Zonal North East India finals, as they saw us as a group and a team up against other teams and they just cheered everyone on. When 13 of the children in the first year got through to the all Indian finals the excitement was unreal with ALL the children, and when they arrived home with a junior All India bronze medal they were total heroes!

One of the girls involved was an eight year old trafficked across the border to Darjeeling. Both her parents were alcoholics and she had been raped and badly abused. She escaped but lived with a woman in a tea garden and was forced to work there by the woman who told her to call her 'mummy'. One day the woman's sister, who had grown fond of the child, heard discussions about selling her to a man in the tea plantation, and brought the child to the Foundation's home. The woman tried to reclaim the child but became frightened when the whole story about the girl was revealed to the police. She became a beautiful confident teenager, took to sports like a duck to water and was one of the first children to enter the North East Zonal competition.

**Edith Wilkins Street Children Foundation, Darjeeling**

The BBC were filming in India for the Sport Relief programme. The comedian, Patrick Kielty, was filmed taking a ten year old boy, Vijay, back to his village after he'd spent two years roaming the Indian railway system, having run away from his impoverished village home. Two years later, for the next Sport Relief telethon, Patrick Kielty was filmed following up his earlier visit to see what had happened to Vijay. They found him at Villupuram railway station in Tamil Nadu and first thought was that he'd run away again. But on closer inspection, the filming team found that he still went to school in the morning and spent the afternoon on the station looking out for runaway children and taking them to the project that had rescued him. Patrick Kielty was reunited with the boy who proudly showed him a badge he wore to give him the authority to be on the station platform. It said 'Social Worker'.

**Vijay, India - Railway Children/Comic Relief**

'I would say that I help people. If someone needs something done or a favour, I would do it for them. Like to send me to buy something or to take care of my brother, I never say no.'

**Street Boy, Morocco - Moroccan Children's Trust**

'I try and help at least one person a day … just sitting down and talking with them or going up to somebody and asking them how they're doing, and I think that has helped me to be an overall better person, be more positive.'

**Street Child, Los Angeles - UN Street Voices Report**

'It's a bit like this: you have to sacrifice things you want for your future, like study maybe, for the future of your family. But, if you ask me, I want to help others. If I am to be asked, what have you done with your life, I want to say that I've helped others. The stuff you do, like giving to those who've been deprived of something, giving them some affection, things like that...'

**Street Girl, Morocco - Moroccan Children's Trust**

'My dream is to change my current situation, to be a father with a good wife and educate my children in the right way so they can be respected and respectful. I wish to become a normal man.'

**Street Boy, Democratic Republic of Congo - UN Street Voices Report**

I want to finish the quotes and stories of the children in this chapter with a story written by the researcher in the Railway Children report on street children's experiences in Kenya and Tanzania, 'Struggling to Survive'. It's about Turusifu, whose desperately sad experiences have been quoted in earlier chapters. The researcher, Emilie Smeaton, said:

'Turusifu has often been beaten and raped whilst living on the streets since the age of ten and it is clear from his description of his early life on the streets that he found it very difficult to adjust to street life and was a victim to the attacks of others. After a brief foray into stealing, Turusifu recognised that this was not something he wanted to continue to do. By the time of his participation in the research, Turusifu's life on the streets had changed in a number of ways as he is the leader of a group of boys who live on the streets and other children listen to him and do as he asks. Turusifu is clearly respected by others in the community such as vendors and the family who feed him and allow him to rest in their house in return for help he provides to them carrying out chores and caring for their children.

As well as carrying out a long and insightful interview, Turusifu acted as guide for the lead researcher, helping her when taking a younger child to hospital and taking two young boys to a centre late one night by finding a taxi driver he knew could be trusted. After hearing the plans of an older boy to attack the researcher, Turusifu made it clear that she was to be left alone and this was adhered to.'

**Turusifu, East Africa – Railway Children**

Working with street children can be both a frustrating and rewarding experience. Children whom you thought were settling down and showing positive signs will suddenly get 'wanderlust' and disappear. Children nursed back to health from injury or illness will one night wave goodbye and not be seen again.

Children you've helped painstakingly to come off drugs will spend one night back on the street with their former friends and next time you see them they're high on solvent once again. A child will come in one night beaten up from a fight with an older youth or an encounter with an insensitive policeman or vicious drug dealer or trafficker.

But for all this frustration there are many rewarding signs of hope. A withdrawn child will suddenly respond to the care and affection shown to them and beam a broad smile at you and begin to talk. A child will one day finally confide in you the truth about their situation and you can begin the healing process. You will see a boy you've provided with a vocational skill proudly show you his first week's wages from the job you helped him get. A former child whom you helped will return after two or three years to show off his young wife and new born child, now off the street and with a modest home. A policeman or a government official will suddenly one day express appreciation for what you are doing.

**Back in 1998, I met a young seven year old girl in a tiny classroom in Howrah on the banks of the Hooghly river opposite Kolkata city. She was one of thirty young girls aged between four and thirteen found sleeping rough on the vast Howrah railway terminus - most had been raped or sexually molested, several were HIV+. We funded a local NGO to hire two social workers as 'aunties' for these girls and a private school who let us use their classroom as a night shelter. Each evening the girls would arrive around 6pm and find a hot meal, a wash and clean clothes awaiting them. After the meal the girls would get health counselling, some basic education, an opportunity to enjoy themselves - they loved dancing - and a safe night's sleep, then at 8am they were back to the street, as the school needed its classroom again. Eventually we leased a home for them and some opted to go to school. The seven year old used to survive by fetching water eight hours every day for local slum families and got paid a rupee a day on which she had to survive before our partner project rescued her. Suddenly ten years later I received a treasured e-mail. It simply said 'Thank you for giving me my childhood back. Love from 'B'.'**

# Chapter 10
## *Bringing about Change*

UN Convention on the Rights of the Child, Article 27:

1) 'State Parties recognize the right of every child to a standard of living adequate for the child's physical, mental, spiritual, moral and social development.

2) The parent(s) or others responsible for the child have the primary responsibility to secure, within their abilities and financial capacities, the conditions of living necessary for the child's development.

3) State parties, in accordance with national conditions and within their means, shall take appropriate measures to assist parents and others responsible for the child to implement this right and shall in case of need provide material assistance and support programmes, particularly with regard to nutrition, clothing and housing.'

**Photograph by David Maidment**

There are no simple solutions. Governments have tried treating street children as delinquents, police have rounded them up, they have been sent to orphanages and other institutions. Children have been sent home, they have been moved on from locations where they have been embarrassments to traders and tourists. And the number of such visible children has not decreased. Children taken from the street soon return when the opportunity exists - they run from institutions, they run from continued abuse, they run from misguided attempts to help by people who lack understanding. They run back to the only friends they knew - the other children on the street. Each street child is an individual with their own history and circumstance, their own personality, fears and hopes. If a real change is to be effected, that fact has to be acknowledged and options found that are appropriate for each child.

Children are on streets for different reasons and need appropriate options and opportunities if any change is to be lasting. Government programmes - when they exist at all - tend to be blunt instruments and often limited to institutional solutions. This is acknowledged by some governments as outdated practice, but too often is still the only state intervention as other solutions are perceived to be complex or require resources that are not available from state agencies. Governments have the duty to create the infrastructure of society that minimises the chances of children needing to turn to the street - or to put it more positively, to create the opportunities for children to develop fully within their families and communities through good health care, education and upholding at least the minimum standard of living as stated in the UN Convention, article 27. Indeed, states have the responsibility of ensuring children are protected, supported and encouraged to reach their potential by ensuring the implementation of all the UN Convention's articles.

A few years ago a British Secretary of State for International Development (Clare Short) met a couple of Board Members and the Director of Consortium for Street Children (CSC) and discussed the role of governments vis à vis street children and gave her opinion that only government agencies could provide the community health, education and family support services required for children generally. This meant that governments were in the key role of 'prevention'. Clare Short identified the role of NGOs working with street children to be twofold - the provision of welfare and development services for children who 'had fallen through the safety net'; and the implementation and evaluation of innovative programmes to support such children that were capable of more widespread replication, possibly with the assistance of state resources.

Most street children still live in their communities for the majority of the time. By definition they spend a considerable portion of the day on the street, unable for various reasons to go to school. They may be neglected, their parents may be away from the home at work or seeking income, they themselves may be looking to earn a few pence by scavenging or other informal activity. They could be labelled as 'children in need of care and protection'. Most children of this ilk are found in the world's city slums. They may be as many as 90% of the world's undetermined number of street children. Whilst, as stated earlier, the prime responsibility for supporting such communities and affording proper health and education facilities falls to the state, many NGOs, including some members of CSC, work with such children and their communities, providing the facilities they can that the state has failed to provide. A number run small slum based non-formal schools, sometimes in partnership with large international NGOs like UNICEF or Save the Children. Many have built relationships with medical staff who will visit such communities on a regular basis to offer their skills to the children free of charge. Some NGOs will develop income generation schemes for the adults and older youth to provide the necessary support to the children; others will help the poorest families by providing school fees or books or uniforms. Some interesting programmes are being developed to work jointly with parents and local communities where such children are at risk, seeking agreed solutions together with all the stakeholders in the area.

Other children at risk, but not yet on the street, are found in rural villages the world over. They may have no opportunity for education; they may be employed in agriculture; they may be existing in families so poor that the children become easy victims of traffickers who offer parents a payment they find hard to refuse and the promise of a job and good future for the child, which is of course a mirage. Again, the chief responsibility for protecting and developing the opportunities for such children belongs to the state. However, increasingly NGOs are developing programmes that raise the awareness of such risks in these rural communities and seek to strengthen the local health and education facilities. A number of NGOs in Northern India are supporting local women's groups or community elders in providing additional school facilities for village children - awareness of their rights and the dangers of street life and trafficking, and recreational facilities that will retain the interest of such children and deter them from seeking adventure on the city streets.

Of course, children of families living in the city slums or even on the street itself, face the dangers of being lured into domestic work or the sex trade or other hazardous occupations. Some NGOs provide drop-in centres for such children so that they are occupied during the day, off the street, receiving basic education, health care and recreation and at least one nutritious meal a day. One social worker from an NGO in Patna (37), in the Indian state of Bihar, told me that she found many young girls hanging round the railway station, children of street living families in the area - but hardly any over the age of ten or so. Were they trafficked? Retained at home for household chores or looking after younger siblings? Or victims of child marriage? Recently (2007) the Indian government enacted a law banning children under the age of 14 from employment in 79 trades, including domestic service. In theory, that state should then ensure children are returned to their families and given educational opportunities. There is a danger that such children, girls in particular, will find their way to even more hazardous occupations such as the sex trade. NGOs are vigilant and monitoring this situation carefully. At present the Act is not being consistently enforced partly because of the lack of state resources to follow it up properly.

A quite different situation exists for children who have left their home for any reason - to seek work, to escape abuse, drifting from neglect or even enticed by the illusory promises of fame and fortune gleaned from TV or an older youth. These children become easy prey for the unscrupulous when they first come to the cities and many NGOs employ street workers to reach out to such children - some around the bus and railway stations where such children first arrive, others in parks and markets where such children congregate. These NGOs offer such facilities as drop-in centres, emergency night shelters, first aid, food and a counselling service seeking to offer the child a way out of his or her situation to a more positive and permanent solution, either reuniting the child with its family and community where this is both practicable and desirable or finding an educational or residential solution where returning home is not an acceptable option. If intervention takes place in the first month of a child coming to the street experience indicates that there is around an 80% chance of a successful positive intervention being made. After six months on the street, this can have fallen to as low as 20%.

A much more difficult group to work with are children who have lived for a number of years on the street and have completely lost contact with their families. These children have formed gangs for their own protection and mutual support; they have developed ways of earning sufficient money for their needs, albeit often at the limits of legality. They are perceived by both the public and the police as feral or delinquent children and are frequently harassed and rejected. They are often high on drugs, inhalants or alcohol. Their future is uncertain - many will succumb to accident injuries or illnesses contracted because of their exposure on the streets. Others will drift into crime, initially as a means of survival, later because they find it brings them a certain status or respect denied to them by the rest of society. Girls and young women in this situation rarely escape from the habits acquired of survival sex and drift into prostitution from which it is hard to escape. Even if they are helped and rehabilitated, there are few communities that will accept them back again because of the stigma attached to their former existence. NGOs working with such children will usually support them where they are - bringing such children into any sort of institution is rarely successful. Key is to provide them with legitimate means of supporting themselves, through vocational training. Many of these children have developed of necessity considerable entrepreneurial skills and these need to be channelled into positive opportunities. The children need help in escaping from their drug and alcohol addictions, they need a mentor whom they can trust and respect, they need an outlet for their energies - often some form of organised sport can be a motivation for these children and young people. Working with such children needs professional skills and considerable perseverance and follow up. But unless the effort is made, society will be the poorer. Crime will increase, more children will be born to children on the street who've little experience of successful parenting and the cycle of neglect, abuse and dysfunction will continue.

Many of these children get arrested by the police for a variety of reasons - petty stealing, fighting, drug related crime - or just loitering and being therefore under suspicion. A number of countries have laws which allow the arrest of children and adults begging, sleeping or loitering in public places. Such children in conflict with the law find themselves frequently as victims of inadequate juvenile justice systems, imprisoned with adults or sent to remand or similar institutions where all too frequently they meet further abuse and violence. Many street children are found to have run from children's homes, orphanages and remand homes - there is evidence that as many as 50% of children found on the streets of Russia and the UK have absconded from such institutions (38). An increasing number of NGOs are finding ways of getting involved in the management of government homes to monitor the implementation of the children's rights in such circumstances. Some are allowed to take education and recreation into these institutions. Others take the most vulnerable children into their residential accommodation. A few NGOs have legal expertise and either work closely with lawyers prepared to work for such children or even establish a legal advocacy section within their own organisation to represent them and also campaign for justice when children have been abused by the authorities. Other NGOs will campaign for children abused by non government agencies and privately run institutions, both secular and religious.

An increasing number of street children are exposed to the HIV/AIDS infection - not just in Africa, but also in Eastern Europe, Latin America and South Asia, because of the risks they run with drug use and their voluntary or involuntary involvement in sexual relationships. In many cases, the infection will not be recognised as these children rarely have health checks, so the infection spreads. Most HIV/AIDS programmes, when they address the vulnerability of children, work through schools and communities, thus missing the most vulnerable children of all - the street children. A few NGOs have obtained funding to run awareness programmes for these children, one or two have even established treatment centres and hospices, especially where the children would otherwise be stigmatised and left to die on the street. CSC has campaigned at international conferences for street children to be included as a priority group within government and international NGO AIDS programmes.

The street children, whose views were sought as part of the report 'Street Voices' to the UN Office of the High Commissioner for Human Rights (OHCHR), made some comments about what they found helpful and their own understanding of their rights:

*'What I'd like is someone who can understand me, someone who can appreciate the work I do, because I feel alone when no-one notices.'*
**Street Girl, Morocco – Moroccan Children's Trust**

*'I would like to say the people who work* (street outreach workers) *are very important to us, the areas they cover and the work they do. First, they give you good bits of advice, they take out of your head all the bad things like drugs, then they teach you, they give you some instruction and teach you literacy, they help you think about your future life. These are the things I think are special about what they do for us.'*
**Street Boy, Democratic Republic of Congo**

*'For me everyone has rights, children, adolescents, older people, adults. They are rights and obligations everyone has.'*
**Street Boy, Ecuador – Juconi**

*'Our teacher doesn't tell us about the rights of the child. But I know that a child is not supposed to work, only when he grows up, then he can work. Then also his parents can't hit him. And also he is not supposed to stay in the street, he is supposed to go to school.'*
**Street Girl, Morocco – Moroccan Children's Trust**

*'Anybody concerned should help me have access and have my rights, but especially my caretakers, NGO, government, police and local councils.'*
**Street Boy, Uganda – Retrak**

*'The person who has all the authority and must make sure that people are aware of their rights is the President of Ecuador... He could make sure that people are aware of their rights, that children know they have real rights, but may not use them or make the most of them. I think that he is the person who can push this forward and he can demand that children's rights are realised. How do these children learn about their rights and how to access them if they are exploited by their own families?'*
**Older Street Boy, Ecuador - Juconi**

A number of individuals from British NGOs working for street children felt the need to combine forces and speak with one voice on behalf of this very marginalised and vulnerable group of children and formed Consortium for Street Children (CSC) in 1992. The then Prime Minister, John Major, launched the new 'umbrella' organisation in 1993 and the original twenty or so members appointed their first full time Director, Anita Schrader, a couple of years later. In the early years CSC developed sharing of information among its network and undertook research and produced booklets on such issues as street children and the law and also on girl street children. In the late 1990s the next Director, Sadia Mahmud-Marshall, spread knowledge of the organisation beyond the UK NGO members and their partners through a series of international conferences in a number of key capital cities in most continents and obtained Comic Relief funding for its development. Director, Alex Dressler, appointed in 2004, grew the membership and initiated a number of joint projects with its members, and obtained funding for what was intended as the first of a series of research reviews of street children on various relevant themes, starting with 'The State of the World's Street Children: Violence', published in 2007. In 2010, the UK based global insurance company, Aviva, adopted street children as it's CSR programme, campaigning under the slogan, 'From Street to School' and supported a number of CSC's members directly in their programmes. As part of its support, Aviva seconded one of its senior managers, Sally Shire, to be Executive Director of the Consortium for the two years 2011-2012.

There are many examples of good practice and innovative programmes undertaken by British NGOs and their overseas local partners. CSC will be aware of these and can signpost anyone interested towards the appropriate project or NGO. The organisation has a small permanent staff and details of its activities and all its current members can be found on its website, www.streetchildren.org.uk. All profits from the publication of this book will go to support CSC and its members.

# Appendix

Many of CSC past and present member organisations have contributed to this book, by providing comments on the chapter content, relevant case histories and photographs. They are all working in the ways described to try to make a difference for the street children of the world - to prevent their numbers increasing through preventative measures, through early outreach and contact, through the provision of short term shelters and welfare, through long term development in education and training, through caring for the most vulnerable in family units and residential homes, seeking to give these children the opportunity they would otherwise never have.

The NGOs who have contributed to this book, their key activities and their contact details, as supplied by the NGOs themselves, are listed below:

### Action for Brazil's Children's Trust:

Supports the work of locally based NGOs in Brazil to help vulnerable children acquire education and skills - also builds confidence and self-belief through drama, dance, film and music.
Website: www.abctrust.org.uk. Tel: 0207 494 9344

### Edith Wilkins Street Children's Foundation:

A Cork based NGO whose founder, Edith Wilkins, is working with sexually abused and trafficked girls in the Darjeeling area of Northern India and adjacent countries. It has a compound of three houses and playground acting as a safe haven for street and trafficked children providing for their physical, emotional and medical needs. There is a girls' half-way house and a boys' night shelter and half-way house with 90 children in these facilities.

There are also two drop-in centres working as launch pads for placing children in schools and vocational training. 200 children have been placed in school or training in the last years. The programme has a multi-functional approach to education incorporating free-play, organised play under the guidance of a psychologist. Website: www.edithwilkins.org.

**Esther Benjamin Trust:**
Works in partnership with the Nepal Child Welfare Foundation with a night shelter for street children and a refuge for children freed from imprisonment with their parents, providing education and vocational training. Seeks to find Nepalese children trafficked to India for circus and domestic work and reunite them with their families in Nepal. Website: www.ebtrust.org.uk E-mail: info@ebtrust.org.uk Tel: 0207 600 5654

**Hope for Children (HOPE):**
HOPE supports small local projects in eight countries and others as the need arises, Helping Orphaned, Poor and Exploited children. This is undertaken through a network of local representatives and partners. Programmes are in Ghana, Zimbabwe, Uganda, Kenya, India, Sri Lanka, Philippines and the UK. The Charity was founded and registered in 1994. Registration number 1041258 Website: www.hope4c.org Email: hope@hope4c.org Tel: 01442 234561
Address: Hope House, 14a Queensway, Hemel Hempstead, Herts HP1 1LR

**International Childcare Trust (ICT):**
Works in partnership with local grassroots NGOs in Africa and Asia - managed and staffed by local people - that protect the rights of some of the most disadvantaged and vulnerable children, many of whom find themselves living and working on the streets where they are vulnerable to violence, abuse and exploitation on a daily basis. ICT and its partners give these children a chance in life by proving temporary shelter, psychosocial support, healthcare, education and training, with the ultimate aim of reuniting them with their families or placing them in a safe and secure home environment. Development House, 56-64 Leonard Street, London EC2A 4LT. Tel: 020 7065 0970, E-mail: info@ict-uk.org, Website: www.ict-uk.org.

**International Children's Trust:**
Supports street children NGOs in Africa and Latin America, the latter through a programme called 'Juconi' in Mexico and Ecuador. Works to rehabilitate street children in an intensive therapeutic way and seeks to prevent children from street living families and

the siblings of street children taking to the street. Website: www.theict.org. Tel: 01733 319777

**Juconi:**
Founded in 1989 with the support of International Children's Trust and local organisations, JUCONI Mexico, (Junto con los Niña/os – Together with the Children), develops, applies and shares solutions for marginalised children, youth and families affected by violence. The Juconi Programme runs 3 educational-therapeutic programmes: for street-living, street-working and market-working children, each including preventive services for siblings at particularly high risk of taking to the street. More than 350 children and 120 families are reached each year, through street-, family- and community-outreach, a residential centre for street-living children, and a day centre for market-working children. A therapeutic programme delivered through weekly home visits to each family is a key element of all Juconi's services. Juconi operates a rigorous monitoring and evaluation system, including a post-graduation tracking programme, and over 80% of participants achieve successful social integration.

Juconi's Technical Support Centre aims to encourage effective programme responses to the complex obstacles faced by children and families affected by violence, particularly street-involved children, in accessing their rights through a) practice-based development of methodologies; b) training and personalised consultancy services for civil society and governmental practitioners in Mexico and internationally, offering practice-based tools for working with vulnerable children; and c) targeted advocacy and collaboration with local and national authorities and NGO networks and d) an on-line resource centre providing access to educational-therapeutic materials from a wide variety of institutions, clinics and programmes from around the world.

Website: **www.juconi.org.mx, www.facebook.com/juconi, www.twitter.com/juconimexico,**. Tel: (00 52 222) 240 8178 / 237 9416

Fundación Juconi AC, 7A Sur 4111, Colonia Gabriel Pastor, Puebla 72420 Mexico

**Jubilee Action:**
Dedicated to rescuing children at risk from abusive situations (slavery, prostitution and illegal imprisonment) and providing them with sustainable solutions for the future. Works in Brazil, Burma, China, Haiti, South Africa, Kenya, the Sudan, Thailand, India and the Philippines. Website: www.jubileeaction.co.uk

**Kidasha** (formerly known as Child Welfare Scheme (CWS)):
Kidasha is a UK-registered charity dedicated to improving equality of opportunity for children in Western Nepal. We deliver access to health and education for mothers and children and protection and support for children who live or work on the street, including those who are commercially sexually exploited. Kidasha has over 15 years of experience and its programme teams are located in Pokhara and made up of locally recruited staff. They have in-depth, first-hand knowledge of the situation on the ground. Further, some of our employees are former beneficiaries with direct experience of the issues we work in. We work in partnership with local communities and organisations and the Nepali government, providing capacity-building support which makes our projects sustainable.

Kidasha works with: children and mothers living in isolated rural communities; children and mothers in urban slums; street and working children and child victims of sexual abuse and exploitation. Our projects range from provision of specific services and immediate support, to addressing the causes of exclusion and vulnerability by influencing policy and practice at both local and national levels. Lack of access to health, education and protection services may be due to geographical barriers or discrimination through gender, disability, caste or religion. Website: www.kidasha.org Tel: UK: +44 (0) 20 7017 8989; Nepal: +977 (0) 61 530 002. E-mail: UK: enquiries@kidasha.org; Nepal: kidasha@kidasha.org

**Railway Children**:
The charity focuses on early intervention to contact runaway and lone street children, if possible before they are traumatised, abused, exploited or corrupted, through 30+ local NGO partners on railway and bus stations in India, East Africa and the UK. Through its partners it provides emergency welfare and protection,

family reintegration and longer term counselling and development support. Railway Children seeks to sensitize communities to the needs of street children and lobby governments for long term positive change.

Website: www.railwaychildren.org.uk.
E-mail: enquiries@railwaychildren.org.uk, Tel: 01270 757596.
Address: 1, The Commons, Sandbach, Cheshire CW11 1EG.

**Retrak:**
Retrak is a UK based charity that works with full time street children in Africa to give them a real alternative to life on the street. Preventative interventions addressing root causes are needed to stop children moving to the streets, but those already on the streets are at high risk, vulnerable and requiring special protection to enable them to develop. It helps them thorough the difficulties that they face each day, getting to know them as individuals and, as trust increases, working with each child on a case by case basis to determine long term and sustainable programmes which will help them discover their self worth and realise their potential.

Retrak's primary goal is to enable street children to return to life in a caring and stable family environment, either with their own family, foster family or by living independently in the community. We work several thousand street children in Africa each year, helping them to achieve their potential and break away from the vicious cycle of poverty and homelessness by providing them with food, temporary shelter & accommodation, catch up education, medical treatment and vocational training. Website: www.retrak.org. E-Mail: mailbox@retrak.org Tel: 0161 486 5104. Address: Landmark House, Station Road, Cheadle Hulme, Cheshire SK8 7BS

**SKCV (Street Kids Community Village):**
Founded in the 1980s by a young man visiting the Hare Krishna movement in Bombay from the UK, SKCV has emergency night shelters and villages for street boys and street girls, providing education, health care and a home in the city and large railway junction of Vijayawada in Andhra Pradesh, India. Website: www.skcv.info, E-mail: headoffice@skcv.info Tel: 0161 973 5042

**Street Child Africa:**
Street Child Africa works with local partner organisations in sub-Saharan Africa to engage and empower children in street situations who are often uncounted and unheard. These children are denied access to education, excluded from healthcare systems, subject to multiple forms of violence and overlooked by national development strategies. Street Child Africa understands that the daily injustices they face are violations of international human rights law: children in street situations are human beings and rights holders entitled to protection, provision of services and participation in matters affecting them.

Street Child Africa funds twelve grassroots organisations that provide family tracing, mediation, reintegration, education, drop-in centres, residential centres and basic healthcare services. Street Child Africa is committed to working in the long-term to: (1) secure funding for the continuous implementation of its partners' project activities, (2) strengthen the capacity of its partner organisations, and (3) raise awareness of the conditions facing children in street situations and the causes leading to these situations in the first place. It accomplishes these goals by fundraising, supporting staff training, project planning, and local and international advocacy work. Street Child Africa's work in Sub Saharan Africa helps children in street situations to realise their rights and their potential. Their potential is our inspiration.

Website: www.streetchildafrica.org.uk. Tel: 0208 972 9820

**Street Kids Direct:**
Street Kids Direct works in partnership with existing projects in Guatemala and Honduras, coming alongside them to provide support, encouragement, training, volunteers, project funding and helping them to network with groups that could help them develop their work. Website: www.streetkidsdirect.org.uk. Tel: 01494 784029

**Street Kids International:**
A Canadian based NGO, registered also in the USA and the UK, that aims to give street children the choices, skills and opportunities to make a better life for themselves. Has worked in over 60 countries. Website: www.streetkids.org

## Toybox

Toybox is a Christian charity committed to working towards a world with no street children. We aim to bring this about by harnessing and collaborating with local people's responses to help the children in their city, working with all children regardless of their faith, gender, ability or background. As well as meeting the urgent needs of children living on the streets, we focus on prevention work with vulnerable children, many of whom work on the streets for a living. We work with families, governments and communities to improve the lives of children. We campaign in Latin America for better access to education, healthcare and other rights for children. Our unique Child Ambassador scheme gives the children a voice in the cities where they live, empowering them to become advocates for change. In the UK we raise awareness and support for street children, influencing the government to prioritise and respond to their situation. We currently work in four countries in Latin America – Guatemala, Bolivia, Peru and El Salvador.

Website: www.toybox.org.uk E-mail: stephen.thorn@toybox.org Tel: 01908 360083.

## Viva a Vida:

A registered charity working in partnership with the non-governmental organisation Viva a Vida located near the city of Salvador, in the northeast of Brazil. Set up in 2005, Viva a Vida was the only therapeutic drug rehabilitation programme for street boys addicted to crack and other drugs in the region. In a participative residential environment, Viva a Vida provided therapeutic as well as educational intervention so that substance-abusing street boys could understand and address their addiction as well as gain the educational tools necessary to build productive lives for themselves once they left the programme. Recognised for its work in drug treatment, Viva a Vida in June 2006 was awarded a Diploma of Merit by the Brazilian governmental National Anti-Drugs Office (SENAD) in a ceremony presided over by the President of Brazil.

Hit hard by the recession and due to progressive funding cuts, Viva a Vida's drug rehabilitation programme had to close its doors in October 2009. However, Viva a Vida continues to run an aftercare support and mentoring service for all those boys who went through the programme as well as a Prevention Project whereby some of the boys from the rehab programme as well as young people from the local community are trained to be peer educators to facilitate HIV/AIDS and substance abuse prevention workshops in schools and community organisations.

Viva a Vida UK, Ronaldsway, Vache Lane, Chalfont St Giles, Bucks. HP8 4SB

Tel: 07719 625 320, info@vivaavida.org www.vivaavida.org

**World Jewish Relief:**

World Jewish Relief (WJR) works primarily in the former Soviet Union and Sub Saharan Africa to provide support to vulnerable communities and individuals. In Rwanda, WJR works with SACCA, a local agency, to help children leave the streets and reintegrate into either their families and/or communities. Work is based in Eastern Province but reintegration and social work also takes social workers into other provinces or countries. Each child is supported on an individual programme, working at his or her own pace and to his or her requirement. While the majority of children are helped to return to school, others prefer to undertake vocational training programmes and informal literacy classes. In 2009, 88 children were living in three centres, 41 youth were living semi-independently and follow-up was being undertaken with 76 children. An additional prevention of separation programme is being undertaken.

In Moldova and Ukraine, the focus is on prevention of separation – working with vulnerable families to ensure that children are able to remain with their families. Support is provided in the form of food and medical provision as well as livelihood support for parents. WJR's livelihood programmes help parents of vulnerable children retrain and regain confidence to enter the work place. For more information, please see www.wjr.org.uk or contact info@wjr.org.uk 0208 7361250.

**Consortium for Street Children**

The Consortium for Street Children (CSC) is the leading international network dedicated to realising the rights of street children worldwide. CSC supports and complements the work of its network members by focusing on four key strategic areas: Advocacy, Research, Shared Learning and Capacity Building. The network is continually expanding and currently there are over 80 members working across 130 countries worldwide. The network comprises small NGOs, multilateral agencies, academics, corporates and individuals, as well as affiliated groups of street children. We believe that collectively we can achieve maximum impact through being 'Louder Together'. www.streetchildren.org.uk.

**What you can do to help**

The first essential, and costing little, is to raise awareness of the issue. Tell your friends. Contact the NGOs and get them to talk to your schools, churches, clubs. If you are in the media, research and write articles for the general public, produce articles and documentaries for newspapers, magazines, radio and TV.

Secondly, the CSC and all the NGOs mentioned need money to carry out their work. It is not cheap, but doing nothing will be even more expensive in time for society, for rejected, bitter or angry children become alienated and open to anti-social activities that cost us all dear. Sometimes a programme to change a child's life can seem remarkably inexpensive - some NGOs in India can provide protection, food, health care, education and a caring environment for not much over £100 per child a year. In the developed world, programmes cost much more - it can cost as much as £5 a call for every child helped on a telephone helpline in Western Europe. But that £5 might make all the difference... These NGOs need sustainable giving wherever possible. Once a programme is started it becomes essential to maintain it for as long as it is effective - for giving a vulnerable child hope and then withdrawing it is doubly damaging.

Thirdly, you can help the CSC and its members' campaign to change the future for street children. The media needs to be stimulated, politicians lobbied. Individual injustices need to be highlighted and pursued until justice is done. Governments need to be challenged when they do not meet their commitments they've made when they signed and ratified the UN Convention on the Rights of the Child. You can do this by supporting the CSC in its advocacy activities or one of its members with an advocacy objective. You can be aware of the situation by becoming a supporter of any of these organisations and using the knowledge you gain to press your local MP, write to your local press, give an interview on a local radio station to publicise a particular pertinent issue.

Finally, you may think the problem is too big. Several times hundreds of thousands of children, if not millions, have been quoted in this book. The problem may seem vast but the solution is child by child. Look at the face of one child helped and take heart from the beaming smile. Once Mother Teresa was asked how her organisation fed and cared for so many children. She answered, 'One at a time'.

# References

1 Research paper 'Off the Radar' on street children in the UK, Emilie Smeaton, Railway Children, 2009
2 Research paper 'Struggling to Survive' on street children in Kenya and Tanzania, Emilie Smeaton, Railway Children, 2012
3 'Children's Voices' paper – findings from consultations with children for the UN Office of the High Commissioner for Human Rights by Anne Louise Meincke, Advocacy Director, Consortium for Street Children, 2012
4 Rees G & Lee J, 2005, 'Still Running 2: Findings from the Second National Survey of Young Runaways.' London: The Children's Society.
5 'State of the World's Children 2011, UNICEF
6 Risk Assessment – Fault & Event Trees of causes and consequences of being a street child, Maidment, Consortium for Street Children, 1993
7 Survey of 1,000 street children in Mumbai, Indian NGO Snehasadan, 1993
8 Amnesty International UK campaign on 'children in conflict situations', 1999
9 Survey by the Municipal Authority of Calcutta, as reported by Indian NGO CINI Asha, Calcutta, 1998
10 Research report by 'Railway Children Russian NGO partner, NAN (No to Alcohol & Narcotics) 'NAN Foundation's Experience in Working with Homeless Children living at Moscow Railway Stations, 2006'.
11 Evidence from the legal office of the NGO 'Casa Alianza' working in a number of Central American national states.
12 'What is and what can be' Multi stakeholder co-operation at railway stations in India for interventions with children in need of care and protection', Railway Children, 2009
13 Situational analyses carried out by Railway Children partners in India at a number of railway stations, 1998-2002.
14 UN Secretary General's Study on 'Violence against Children', by Independent Expert, Professor Paulo Sergio Pinheiro, 2006
15 Research report commissioned by the UN Office of the Human Rights Commissioner, by Dr Sarah Thomas de Benitez, 2011.
16 Amnesty International action cases on street children in Brazil

and other Central American republics, 1990-1993, in conjunction with NGO Casa Alianza.

17 'A Study on Child Abuse' commissioned by the India Government Department of Women & Child Development, 2007

18 Bal Sakha, Patna (Bihar) and Jeevodaya, Itarsi (Madhya Pradesh), partners of Railway Children

19 The essay in this chapter is drawn from the same material as the chapter on 'Worst Forms of Child Labor – Street Children & Street Trades', Maidment 2008, from the book 'The World of Child Labor – an Historical and Regional Survey" edited by Hugh D Hindman and published by ME Sharpe Inc, USA 2009.

20 New Hope, Visakhapatnam, partner of Railway Children

21 'Pintesh', from 'Sarjan, Ahmedabad, a partner NGO of 'Railway Children'

22 Evidence from 'Casa Alianza' in Central America, New Hope in Andhra Pradesh, India.

23 Railway Children working with its partner 'Project Concern International' in Nizamuddin, Delhi, funded by the Elton John Foundation, to train staff from Railway Children's other Indian NGO partners.

24 Evidence from 'Stepping Stones Nigeria' and 'Warchild' in the Democratic Republic of Congo.

25 'Casa Alianza' in Guatemala, Nicaragua and Honduras.

26 'Butterflies', New Delhi, partner of Railway Children

27 'Sarjan' Ahmedabad, India

28 'M'Lop Tapang, partner of International Children's Trust

29 'Cosmos', partner of Railway Children

30 'CSKS', Dacca, partner of Methodist Relief & Development Fund and Railway Children

31 'SKCV' at Vijayawada railway junction, partner of Railway Children

32 'Jeevodaya', Itarsi railway junction

33 'Project Mainstream', Mumbai

34 'Undugu Society', Nairobi, partner of Railway Children

35 'Edith Wilkins Street Children Foundation', Cork and Darjeeling

36 'Sport–For-Development Impact Study', Comic Relief and UK Sport, Professor Fred Coalter, October, 2010

# Postscript

*Quotations from young people who'd lived for more than a month on the streets of the UK, when asked for suggestions to help children like themselves:*

'Comfort them; talk to them; give them something to eat. Talk to them; see how they're feeling. If you can't do anything to help them, make them comfy and wish them luck...'

'There should be more support put in place for kids. Like, social workers and stuff need to realise that they've got to listen to the kids and not make judgments for them 'cos every time I saw a social worker, they didn't listen to what I wanted.'

'Kids need to be taught how to look after themselves and not how to put themselves at risk. They (social workers) always tell you 'you're putting yourself at risk' but they never tell you how not to. They never ask you why you're doing it and what's causing it.'

'Just people, basically, to listen to them. I've basically learnt, right, over the years, that the best form of help is, when I'm angry or hurt, for someone to say 'listen, I'm hear to listen to you and I'm not going to tell you what to do or what you cannae do. I'm not going to tell you if you're in the wrong. I'm just here to listen to you. Do you know what I mean? I don't think I'd have been so violent or angry if there had been someone like that for me.'

Let the last word go to the street girl whose words were quoted at the beginning of this book and inspired its title:
'You've already helped me. You're the first person in my life who's ever listened to me.'
**UK – 'Off the Radar' research report, Railway Children**